Experts Answer
101 Tough Practice Management Questions

Compiled by
Mary Mourar, MLS

Edited by
Kenneth T. Hertz, CMPE
Cynthia L. Dunn, FACMPE
Nick A. Fabrizio, PhD, FACMPE
Jeffrey B. Milburn, MBA, CMPE

Medical Group Management Association
104 Inverness Terrace East
Englewood, CO 80112-5306
877.275.6462
Website: www.mgma.com

Medical Group Management Association (MGMA) publications are intended to provide current and accurate information and are designed to assist readers in becoming more familiar with the subject matter covered. Such publications are distributed with the understanding that MGMA does not render any legal, accounting, or other professional advice that may be construed as specifically applicable to an individual situation. No representations or warranties are made concerning the application of legal or other principles discussed by the authors to any specific factual situation, nor is any prediction made concerning how any particular judge, government official, or other person will interpret or apply such principles. Specific factual situations should be discussed with professional advisors.

Production Credits

Editorial Director: Marilee E. Aust
Project Editor: Anne Serrano, MA
Page Design, Composition and Production: Kurtz Communications
Copy Editor: Franklin S. Kurtz, Kurtz Communications
Proofreader: Mara G. Gaiser
Cover Design: Ian Serff, Serff Creative Group, Inc.

Library of Congress Cataloging-in-Publication Data

Mourar, Mary.
  Experts answer : 101 tough practice management questions / compiled by Mary Mourar ; edited by Kenneth T. Hertz ... [et al.].
  p. ; cm.
  Includes bibliographical references.
  Summary: "This collection offers the 101 most frequently asked questions received by MGMA's Information Center and experts' answers to them. Topics include requests from the history of medical group practice as well as questions that deal with current issues and emerging trends from business operations to human resources to strategic planning"--Provided by publisher.
  ISBN 978-1-56829-280-9
  1. Medicine--Practice--Miscellanea. I. Hertz, Kenneth T., CMPE. II. Medical Group Management Association. III. Title.
  [DNLM: 1. Practice Management, Medical. W 80 M929e 2007]
  R728.M667 2007
  610.68--dc22

                                                                    2007001905

Item #6661

ISBN-13: 978-1-56829-280-9

Copyright © 2007 Medical Group Management Association

All rights reserved. No part of this publication may be reproduced, stored in a retrieval system or transmitted, in any form or by any means, electronic, mechanical, photocopying, recording or otherwise, without the prior written permission of the copyright owner.

Printed in the United States of America

10 9 8 7 6 5 4 3 2 1

CONTENTS

PREFACE	v
INTRODUCTION	1
CHAPTER 1: Business and Clinical Operations	3
CHAPTER 2: Financial Management	31
CHAPTER 3: Governance and Organizational Dynamics	73
CHAPTER 4: Human Resources Management	97
CHAPTER 5: Information Management	147
CHAPTER 6: Planning and Marketing	179
CHAPTER 7: Professional Responsibility	211
CHAPTER 8: Risk Management	235
INDEX	271

PREFACE

A Day in the Life

Each day, the MGMA Information Center fields dozens of phone calls and e-mails from MGMA members. The MGMA librarians offer research services – at no charge – for those administrators and executives who find themselves unable to find the answer to their most pressing questions.

Of course, each question is unique, as this example illustrates:

> Almost any day of the week, we can find Doug at his desk, sipping coffee and surfing through today's health care news. His phone rings. His chipper voice resounds through the walls of his cubicle, "Good morning, MGMA Information Center, Doug speaking."
>
> "Hi, this is Terry from ABC Medical Practice in Maintown, Ohio. My MGMA member number is R10755, and I'm hoping you can help me with another question."
>
> "Hi Terry. Sure thing. Let me give it a shot."
>
> "I'm looking for a template of a letter to send to patients when a physician is leaving the practice. Do you have anything like that?"
>
> "You bet. If you'll give me your e-mail address, I'll send you a sample letter and checklist for physicians who are leaving a practice."
>
> Terry is thrilled. "Thanks!"
>
> Doug sits back, starts reading an article on HSAs when the phone rings again. "Good morning, MGMA Information Center, Doug speaking."

"Hi, Doug. About eight months ago the administrator who worked here before I came on board downloaded a new physician checklist/mentoring list off of the MGMA Website. I've been looking online and can't find anything that comes close to what my physician remembers. He recalls that it had recommended dates to review certain issues like practice expectations, patient volume, and other issues. Do you think you can help me out in locating this form?"

"No problem. You can find that at mgma.com/forms."

Doug checks his e-mail, finding a question from Marie in New England. She wants to know what other pediatric practices are finding as the most profitable ancillary services ... and Doug begins another search.

You see, Doug and his colleagues answer hundreds of questions each week. Thus, we've compiled the most frequently asked questions in this guide just for you!

If you don't find the answer to your question within these pages, we encourage you to reach out to the staff members at MGMA's Information Center or to the expert consultants in the MGMA Health Care Consulting Group. Simply dial, toll-free, 1-877-275-6462.

INTRODUCTION

Since its founding in 1972, the library at the Medical Group Management Association (MGMA) has been the information resource for professionals in medical practice management. Practice executives, administrators, physicians, and others have turned to the MGMA librarians for help in dealing with practice management issues. Requests for information have been as simple as "What is the average operating cost for my specialty?" and as complex as "What can I do for my practice to succeed in this changing health care environment?"

The MGMA librarians are adept at answering questions dealing with all aspects of medical practice management, from business operations to human resources to strategic planning. They have helped with issues representing ongoing concerns (such as financial ratios) and emerging trends (including physician pay for performance). Whether a request for information arrives via phone or e-mail, the librarians draw on a variety of resources to provide an answer, from MGMA's survey reports or Center for Research results, to industry consultants and think tanks, and the collection of industry literature and Internet resources.

Gathered here for the first time is a collection of 101 of the most frequently asked questions received by the MGMA Information Center, which was formerly known as the MGMA Library. Included are information requests from throughout the history of medical group practice as well as questions that deal with current issues and emerging trends. The questions were compiled, researched, and answered, and then reviewed by the experts in the MGMA Health Care Consulting Group for content, validity, and accuracy.

Arrangement of the 101 questions is by competency domain as identified in the Body of Knowledge for Medical Practice Management, developed by The American College of Medical Practice Executives, the certification body of MGMA. The domains are:

1. Business and Clinical Operations;
2. Financial Management;
3. Governance and Organizational Dynamics;
4. Human Resources Management;
5. Information Management;
6. Planning and Marketing;
7. Professional Responsibility; and
8. Risk Management.

Every medical practice executive will find answers to some very pressing and frequently asked questions of their colleagues. Executives will also glean knowledge and resources from this title, either for help with an existing issue in the practice or for a problem that might soon require a response.

CHAPTER 1

Business and Clinical Operations

CHAPTER 1: Business and Clinical Operations

QUESTION 1

What methodologies are other practices using to reduce the number of patient no-shows and late cancellations? Can we charge a patient a no-show charge?

Practices that track no-shows and cancellation rates averaged 5 percent no-shows and cancellations, according to an MGMA *Information Exchange* (an informal survey with voluntary participation). To reduce the number of no-shows, they used the following patient appointment reminder techniques:

- 75.7 percent have staff make telephone calls;
- 19.3 percent send postcards/mailers;
- 18.8 percent have an automated attendant system make calls; and
- 5.9 percent have a vendor handle reminders and confirmations.

When patients miss an appointment:

- 69.8 percent of practices do not charge the patient;
- 9.8 percent charge only for chronic cancellers and no-shows;
- 8.4 percent charge for the appointment (75 percent of these charge a flat fee rather than the full appointment charge); and
- 6.5 percent charge after one missed appointment.

Elizabeth Woodcock, MBA, FACMPE, CPC, in the book *Mastering Patient Flow,* offers the following suggestions to reduce the number of no-shows:

- ➤ Develop strong relationships with patients to increase their commitment to your practice. Suggestions include sending birthday or holiday cards and assigning nurses to specific patients to work and follow up with.

- ➤ Schedule appointments within a reasonable time of the patient's call. The longer the lapse, the greater the chance of a no-show.

- ➤ Switch to open or advanced access scheduling to provide appointments the same day a patient is looking for an appointment (see Question #8).

- ➤ Remind patients of their appointment and ask them to confirm their commitment to the appointment;

- ➤ Monitor your no-shows. Are they more apt to be covered by one insurance carrier, seen on a particular day of the week or by one physician, or is there some other factor that prevents them from honoring their appointment?

- ➤ Develop a policy for dealing with repeat offenders. Specify how future appointments will be handled.

Charging patients who miss appointments may not be the best policy, especially for first-time offenders. It may cost the practice more to bill the patients than the amount to be collected, and patients may choose to leave the practice. Other options include: contacting the patient for reasons for missed appointments and reiterating the value of the physician's scheduled time; scheduling repeat offenders at times that will be less of an impact to the practice, including double scheduling their time; and discharging the patient after multiple no-shows with attempts by the practice to contact the patient. Whatever policy your practice develops, make sure that it is widely publicized to all patients.

Sources:

Medical Group Management Association, "Patient No-Shows and Cancellations," *Information Exchange* #4574 (Englewood, CO: Medical Group Management Association, July 2005.

Mike Norbut, "Nabbing No-Shows: What Can You Do When Patients Are Absent?" *American Medical News*, V. 47, No. 41, November 1, 2004, www.ama-assn.org/amednews (accessed July 15, 2006).

Elizabeth Woodcock, *Mastering Patient Flow: More Ideas to Increase Efficiency and Earnings*, 2nd Edition (Englewood, CO: Medical Group Management Association, 2003).

QUESTION

What are the key areas of assessment that I should track in our practice? What tools are available to help?

Financial assessments are discussed in Question #23 (Financial Management, Chapter 2). However, it is also important to track several nonfinancial areas to ensure a successful practice.

Practice consultant Elizabeth Woodcock's recommendations for monitoring practice operations include the following:

> ➤ **Patient satisfaction** – Has a survey been conducted recently, and have issues been addressed?

> ➤ **Patient access** – What is the wait time for the next available appointment? Are physicians reaching or exceeding national benchmarks for the number of visits per day?

> ➤ **Space utilization** – Are appointments delayed because of a lack of space? Are exam rooms underutilized?

An excellent tool for conducting practice assessments is the *Assessment Manual for Medical Groups*, edited by Darrell Schryver. Available from MGMA, this publication walks you through the internal and external environments, the financial picture, and all operational aspects of your medical group.

The *Assessment Manual* suggests monitoring the following areas related to patient access and services in your practice:

- Compare and evaluate the current typical appointment wait time. Does it show an increased demand for one service or a decline in another? Is the wait time long enough to affect patient satisfaction?

- What have been the factors in deciding whether to add new services or expand current services, including adding more providers?

- What were the financial, personnel, and spatial constraints that limited the expansion of services?

- Are there cultural or language barriers that limit patients' access to services?

- Are there physical barriers, including the practice's location or proximity to parking, that limit patients' access to service?

- Do inefficient appointment scheduling and follow-up care create barriers?

- Are you a patient-oriented group?

- Does the clinical and administrative personnel mix still support the service demand in your practice? Have there been changes in personnel when the services changed?

After conducting a practice audit, you will be able to identify areas of concern and areas to concentrate on for improvement. Balanced scorecards are tools for monitoring the areas for improvement and their selected performance indicators. Performance goals are identified for each area and displayed along with current measures for the indicators. The performance wheel is modified over time to display the

CHAPTER 1: Business and Clinical Operations

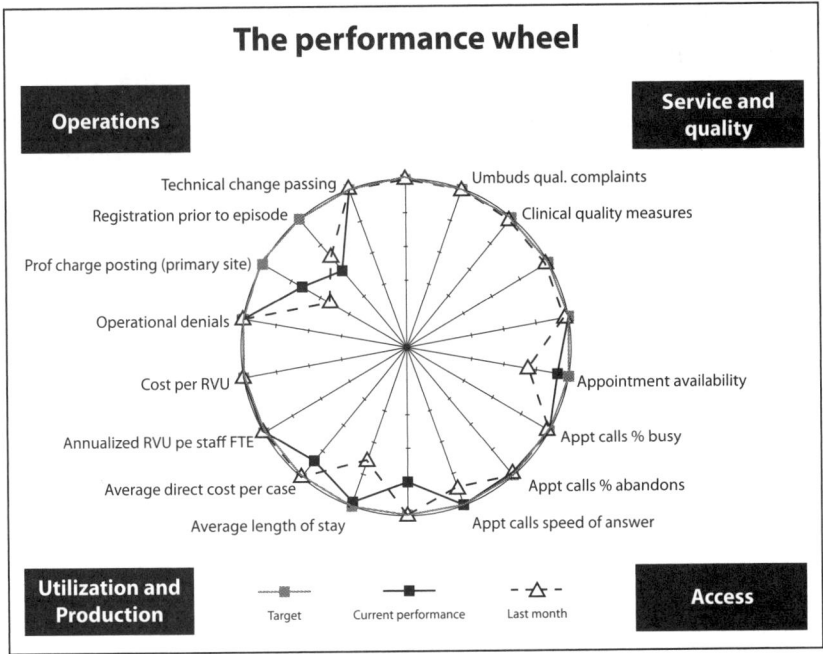

improvements made in reaching the goals, providing an easy way to identify areas still needing attention.

One example of a performance wheel is the one developed by the Cleveland Clinic Foundation (CCF), which displays key indicators identified by the practice. The CCF supplements the performance wheel with tables showing the goals and measures along with comments related to the indicator and plans for reaching the goal. The practice felt the balanced scorecard was an easy way to motivate employees and show progress toward reaching the goals.

Sources:

Elizabeth Woodcock, "Practice Benchmarking," in *Physician Practice Management: Essential Operational and Financial Knowledge,* edited by Lawrence F. Wolper (Sudbury, MA: Jones and Bartlett Publishers, 2005).

Robert Kay, Tina Kaatz, Marty Sargeant, Muzaffar Ahmad, and James Stoller, "Balancing the Perfect Scorecard: Inquiry as Intervention in Physician Practice Management," *MGM Journal,* V. 47, No. 5, September 2000.

Darrell Schryver, editor, *Assessment Manual for Medical Groups,* 4th Edition (Englewood, CO: Medical Group Management Association, 2002).

QUESTION 3

What criteria should I use for deciding when to add a physician to my practice? How do I determine if we should hire a physician or nonphysician provider to handle our demand?

The decision to hire a new provider should be based on many criteria. Recruiting, training, and covering the provider's expenses for the first year will require a fair amount of investment from your practice.

However, there will come a time when your current physicians' patient panels are too large and patients have to wait too long for the next available appointment. If patients are waiting four weeks or longer for an appointment, they may start looking for another physician. If physicians are increasing their workload to cover increasing patient demand, they could suffer from overload and burnout. If the number of patients and patient visits greatly exceed the medians

---

A CLOSER LOOK...

Median number of patients per FTE physician

Specialty	Patients	Encounters
Family practice	2,446	5,891
Obstetrics and gynecology	2,169	6,005
Pediatrics	2,508	6,491
Cardiology	1,461	5,322
Gastroenterology	1,849	3,656
Orthopedic surgery	1,405	4,023
Urology	2,020	4,709

Patients = The number of individual patients who received services from the practice during the reporting year.

Encounters = The number of documented face-to-face contacts between patients and a provider during the reporting year.

Source: Medical Group Management Association, *Cost Survey for Single-Specialty Practices: 2005 Report Based on 2004 Data* (Englewood, CO: Medical Group Management Association, 2005).

in the MGMA *Cost Survey Report* (see "A Closer Look") and the MGMA *Physician Compensation and Production Survey*, it may be time to take action.

There may also be opportunities to expand your practice by offering additional services to meet changing patient demands or to limit the number of referrals to other physicians. A new physician may be needed to provide the new service or take some of the patients of a current physician who will provide the new service.

The following questions can help you determine whether a new physician is needed:

- ➤ Will a nonphysician provider serve your needs? Do physicians currently provide services to patients that a nurse practitioner or physician assistant could provide? Could hiring additional RNs and assigning them tasks related to patient flow relieve the physicians and allow them [the physicians] to handle more patients?

- ➤ Is the practice prepared for the investment of funds needed to recruit and pay a new provider until enough new revenue is generated? (See Question #14 for more guidance on this issue.)

- ➤ Is there enough physical space for an additional physician? You will need space for an office and one or two exam rooms. One way to handle this is to extend office hours and have early and late schedules. There will still be overlap during the middle of the day.

- ➤ Will additional staff be needed, and is there space?

Sources:

"Find Out Now If You Need to Recruit a Doctor," *The Physician's Advisory*, V. 100, No. 2, February 2000.

Anita J. Slomski, "When to Hire Another Doctor – And How to Make It Pay," *Medical Economics*, V. 77, No. 13, July 10, 2000.

Ken Terry, "Adding a Doctor? Ask These Questions," *Medical Economics*, March 18, 2005, www.memag.com/memag/article/articleDetail.jsp?id=151138 (accessed July 19, 2006).

QUESTION 4

We need to expand to a larger facility. Is it better to lease or own our new office space?

There are pros and cons for both leasing and owning your medical office and several questions to consider in helping you decide what's best for your practice at this time.

Advantages of owning your own office space include:

➤ Increased control over the space with no concern that the landlord will change, increase the rent, or want to convert the property to another use;

➤ Control over decisions related to capital improvements and renovations;

➤ Benefits of equity appreciation in the real estate market; and

➤ Tax benefits with deductions related to interest and property taxes and depreciating the capital improvements on the property.

Disadvantages of building ownership include:

➤ Difficulty in selling a medical practice building if the practice breaks up or closes;

➤ Less flexibility to meet changing demands or changes in the surrounding location because ownership may keep your practice in the same facility longer than if you were leasing;

➤ Time and resource commitment to maintaining the building and managing capital improvements that the landlord or property manager would otherwise handle;

- Committing the capital to facility purchase rather than to growing the practice or investing in needed information technology or other business expenses; and

- Handling the issues related to structuring the ownership and financing of the facility. These issues, if not addressed during the decision-making process, could result in disgruntled and dissatisfied partners/physicians.

If you decide to purchase the facility, it is not recommended that the purchase occur through the current medical practice entity. Instead create a real estate partnership, corporation, limited liability company, or limited liability partnership for ownership. The advantages of a separate entity include the following:

- Medical practice financial statements and tax returns can be separated from the real estate ownership;

- The allocation of earnings from the practice can be managed differently from the allocation of profits and tax benefits of the property; and

- The buy-in and buyout of the real estate entity can be separated from the practice partnership, a potential issue for new physicians or retiring physicians.

Questions you should consider before making the decision include:

- How long will the practice want to be at the new location? Will the new location remain desirable, or will changes in the surrounding community affect your practice?

- Will the practice continue to grow and need more space in the foreseeable future? It may be easier to move again rather than add to a purchased facility.

➤ What is the current rental market? Are there facilities available for rent/lease that match your needs in your desired location? Are rates favorable?

➤ Will the purchase divert funds needed for other business expenses?

Sources:

Julie A. Jacob, "Factors to Weigh When Deciding Whether to Buy or Rent," *American Medical News*, V. 44, No. 13, April 2, 2001.

Kathleen McKee, "Own Your Office? What to Consider," *Medical Economics*, December 16, 2005, www.memag.com/memag/article/articleDetail.jsp?id=257391 (accessed July 12, 2006).

"Ownership of the Office Facility: An Introduction to Real Estate Partnerships," *On Managing*, V. 14, No. 2, February 2004.

QUESTION 5

My practice seems to be experiencing a high rate of patient turnover, but I don't know what to compare my numbers with. Does MGMA have information on patient retention rates?

There are no current studies on average patient retention or turnover rates. The average turnover rate is thought to be 10 percent to 20 percent of patients each year. High percentages are found in areas of high managed care and more transient populations. Some consultants recommend that you plan on a 20 percent new-patient ratio to replace patients who will be leaving your practice. The new patients will also help the practice maintain higher reimbursement due to higher charges for new patients. The ability to attract and add new patients to the practice depends on providing *visibly* good-quality service.

If your practice has a higher-than-average turnover rate, you should investigate the cause. It may be due to factors out of your control, including a transient patient population that changes physicians when they move or change jobs. However, patients are more likely to change physicians if they are dissatisfied with your practice or the physicians.

You may want to ask departing patients the reason for their departure or conduct a patient satisfaction survey to identify areas of concern.

According to an online survey, the top five reasons for changing physicians were:

- ➤ The physician was not covered by the patient's health plan;
- ➤ The patient moved to another location;
- ➤ The patient didn't like the physician's style, manner, or personality;
- ➤ The patient didn't have confidence in the physician's medical skills; and
- ➤ The patient needed a doctor with a different specialty.

Ideas that practices have implemented to retain patients include the following:

- ➤ Increasing physician time with patients;
- ➤ Increasing patient flow and improving the scheduling system to reduce patient wait time;
- ➤ Returning messages and contacting the patient with test results in a reasonable time;
- ➤ Providing customer relation and patient satisfaction training for staff and physicians; and
- ➤ Developing a relationship or connection with patients by remembering details of patients' history, family, and so on.

Sources:

"Three More Ways to Measure Your Practice Management Vital Signs," *Conomikes Reports*, V. 20, No. 7, February 2001.

Roberta Clarke, MBA, DBA, "Costs and Prevention of Patient Defection," *Journal of Medical Practice Management*, V. 17, No. 1, July/August 2001.

"Online Survey, Few Patients Switch Doctors after Shabby Treatment," *Wall Street Journal*, February 5, 2003, online.wsj.com (accessed February 25, 2003).

QUESTION 6

I know that MGMA studies practices that are classified as better performers. Is there a common theme in what these practices are doing that leads to their success?

Each year, MGMA examines the data reported by medical groups in the MGMA *Cost Survey Report* to identify practices demonstrating superior financial performance. The results appear in the annual *Performance and Practices of Successful Medical Groups* report.

The performance information and, more importantly, the success stories of individual medical groups selected as better performing practices show that these organizations have much in common, including:

➤ A culture that focuses on the patient and providing high-quality services, shown by the frequency in which they conduct patient satisfaction surveys;

➤ An emphasis on increasing productivity from both physicians and staff, even if it involves higher operat-

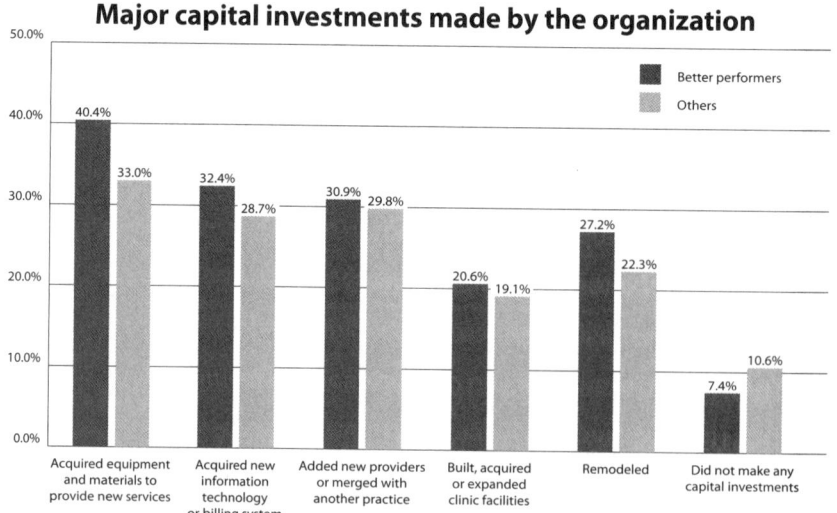

ing costs to invest in the resources needed to maximize physician productivity;

➤ Physician compensation systems based on productivity; and

➤ A willingness to invest in their future through capital expenditures such as new equipment to provide new services, information technology, or new facilities.

Performance indicators for multispecialty practices

	Better performers	Others
Total gross charges per FTE physician	$1,451,171	$1,057,233
Total RVUs per FTE physician	13,870	12,288
Total support staff per FTE physician	5.7	5.1
Total medical revenue per FTE physician	$854,935	$678,409
Total operating cost per FTE physician	$512,385	$399,752
Total medical revenue after operating cost per FTE physician	$362,660	$273,037

Note: FTE = full-time-equivalent; RVUs = relative value units

This table shows accomplishments of the better-performing practices in productivity, capacity, and staffing compared with responding medical groups that did not meet the performance criteria. The data trends are evident. The better performers had substantially greater productivity, higher employee staffing ratios, and higher costs than the other medical groups. Their investments in staff, facilities, and technology paid off in higher productivity, higher medical revenue, and more profit (total medical revenue after operating cost per full-time-equivalent [FTE] physician).

Better-performing medical practices stand out for their management and how they think; governance of the day-to-day issues is vested with a strong physician-administrator team. This type of governance facilitates decision making, allowing the organization to act in a more timely fashion, furthering its ability to compete. The physician-administrator team is accountable to the physicians as a whole, but the need for consensus regarding routine decisions is not the standard.

These organizations achieve success by focusing on the patient and maximizing productivity. They invest in their futures by adding facilities and services that meet patients' needs and by staffing at a level that allows physicians to be more productive. The result is higher revenue for the practice.

Source:

David N. Gans, "On the Edge: Better-Performing Medical Groups. How Do They Do It?" *MGMA Connexion*, V. 6, No. 2, February 2006.

QUESTION 7

Can you advise us on how to evaluate patient flow and implement changes for improvement?

Patient flow is a complex process that encompasses everything from the patient's appointment request, patient check-in, the provision of patient care, and patient checkout. It involves the participation of and communication among many employees and providers. An efficient patient flow is a factor in maintaining patient satisfaction and a successful practice.

All medical practices should have written operating policies and procedures. This documentation allows the employer to communicate with staff consistently regarding the medical practice's expectations of them. The philosophy of how the medical practice handles patients and operational flow is an invaluable tool for all employees.

Because of the complexity of patient flow, we'll touch on just one aspect here, the checkout process with advice provided in the book *Mastering Patient Flow: More Ideas to Increase Efficiency and Earnings,* 2nd Edition. A smooth checkout

> **KEY POINT**
>
> *All medical practices should have written operating policies and procedures. This documentation allows the employer to communicate with staff consistently regarding the medical practice's expectations of them.*

process ensures proper communication with patients about payment and reduces the number of follow-up calls from patients.

As patients depart, they should receive the following items, as appropriate:

- Follow-up scheduling;
- Outbound referrals and ancillary care;
- Payment information;
- Educational materials; and
- Prescriptions.

It is best to ask for payment during check-in. Instruct staff members to request payment politely but firmly, and be sure your organization can accept credit cards, debit cards, and personal checks, as well as cash.

To prevent charge tickets from getting misplaced, ensure that the staff has already collected all of them by the end of each patient's visit, as well as any outstanding balances that may have slipped through previously. This means that every physician must complete his or her patients' charge tickets at the end of each encounter, rather than at the end of the day. Employees can either enter charges into the practice management system as patients leave or later in the day, as time permits. Alternatively, staff members can gather charge tickets, check them, and run batch totals. Regardless of which system your group uses, accuracy is paramount.

Use an encounter form that has a place for the physician to indicate if and when a patient should schedule a follow-up visit. Checkout employees can then help patients make appointments and provide confirmation on a reminder card.

If departing patients need referrals to specialists or ancillary services, your practice can:

- Give patients the necessary referral paperwork in the exam room; patients then go to a counter where an employee processes it and/or schedules the appointment;
- Conduct the referral and scheduling process in the exam room;
- Conduct the referral and scheduling process at the nurses' station; or
- Process referrals and insurer authorizations automatically.

Give patients educational materials at checkout if they have not already received them from the nursing staff. Have your checkout staff ask patients if they have questions about their prescriptions.

Some practices are choosing to move some if not all checkout procedures closer to the clinical area and away from the check-in/reception area. This decision may be prompted by the demands of your group's specialty, but practices that decentralize the checkout process conclude patients' visits more quickly. These organizations typically use "care teams" – physicians, clinical assistants, and clerical employees – to provide care and explain follow-up activities to patients.

By ending your patients' visits efficiently, you send them off on a positive note and reduce the workload in your office.

Source:
Lisa H. Schneck, "Digest: How Efficient is Your Checkout Process?" *MGMA e-Connexion*, March 2004.

 QUESTION 8

I'm thinking of revamping the appointment system in my practice. I'd like to learn more about advanced access and how to implement it.

Advanced access, previously known as "open access," is a system that is patient centered rather than physician or practice centered. Its precepts are:

➤ Patients will be seen by a provider when they want to be seen rather than at "the next available appointment"; and

➤ Patients will see their provider of choice.

Advanced access focuses on maximizing a practice's daily capacity to meet the demand for care, providing same-day appointments, eliminating the backlog of appointments and crowded waiting rooms, and increasing the opportunity for patients to see their own physicians.

To achieve advanced access, you must first determine your appointment capacity (the number of appointments per day) and calculate the demand for services (the number of appointment requests plus walk-ins). Once advanced access is implemented, physicians should begin each day with only 25 percent to 30 percent of their appointment slots filled, leaving the rest of the day to see patients with immediate needs.

Your practice's backlog of patient appointments must then be reduced. You may have to increase capacity for a time, extending office hours, hiring temporary employees, or adding appointments to each day. Decrease the types of appointments, or schedule appointments only by time (long or short). Begin reducing the number of future appointments, encouraging patients to visit on that day instead.

The final step is to work with patients to reduce the number of visits. Offer patients options other than face-to-face appointments with physicians when these are not necessary – for example, to have their questions answered, obtain prescriptions, acquire self-care and self-management skills, and learn about their health conditions. Consider using physician extenders, offering telephone information services, disseminating information online and by e-mail, and institute a program of group visits and drop-in group medical appointments.

By implementing advanced access through predicting demand and reshaping your capacity to meet it, your medical practice can reap the rewards of happier patients, a more efficient operation, and improvements to the bottom line.

Source:

Lisa H. Schneck, "Know How: Open-Access Scheduling Can Open the Door to Better Performance," *MGMA Connexion*, V. 1, No. 1, September 2001.

We recently conducted a patient satisfaction survey and found that there is some dissatisfaction related to patient communication, especially with our phone service. Do you have advice on how we can improve our telephone operations?

There are several issues that could adversely impact your practice's telephone connection with your patients. You will need to analyze your current service to find out what is causing the patients' unhappiness.

To diagnose the problem, you may want to conduct more detailed patient surveys, interview individual patients, conduct a patient focus group, or have an employee or a contracted "mystery patient" call the practice from the outside numerous times. Also, gather information on call volume, hold time, number of hang-ups, and related items from your current telephone service provider and phone system. Your employees may have insight into what could be improved.

Telephone-related issues that cause patient dissatisfaction include being transferred too many times, not having their calls returned in a timely manner, having a confusing automated system, being put on hold for too long, and dealing with rude employees.

The solutions for improving your phone service will depend on the problems you identify. If hold time is too long, consider implementing an automated system that directs patients to the department they need. Make sure that the personnel in those departments are available to answer calls or a process is in place to return calls in a timely manner. To manage patient expectations, provide estimates to the caller on the time required to return calls (e.g., "Calls received before 2:30 p.m. are returned the same business day"). If the automated system is too complicated, work with employees and the system vendor on ways to simplify it. Provide customer service training for employees who answer phones and have contact with patients. Train your employees to understand practice operations to reduce the number of transfers.

New, advanced phone systems offer features that can address several potential concerns. Some of the features that are now available to improve your system include:

➤ Voice response unit;

➤ Messaging and paging;

➤ Reporting packages, real-time and historical;

➤ Voice mail;

➤ Automatic appointment reminders;

- Appointment/procedure scheduling;
- Class registration; and
- Customer relations management.

A phone call is usually the first contact that patients have with your practice. Don't make it their last.

Sources:

Ariana Harner, "Know-How: Phone Talk: The Human Side of Call Management," *MGMA Connexion*, V. 2, No. 3, March 2002.

Ariana Harner, "Know-How: End Telephone System Hassles Before They Hang Up Your Practice," *MGMA Connexion*, V. 2, No. 8, September 2002.

QUESTION 10

Several of my physicians are complaining that our facility isn't big enough. What resources are available for comparing square footage, number of exam rooms, and other facility data for medical practices?

MGMA offers three resources with information on facilities of medical group practices:

1. *Information Exchange* #3410, "Space Planning," is an informal questionnaire asking medical groups about their number and size of exam and treatment rooms. The results from the questionnaire show that the

---

FOR MORE INFORMATION...

Three important resources that have information on managing medical group practice facilities:

- ✔ MGMA's *Information Exchange* #3410, "Space Planning"
- ✔ MGMA's annual *Cost Survey Report*
- ✔ *Medical and Dental Space Planning: A Comprehensive Guide to Design, Equipment, and Clinical Procedures,* 3rd Edition, by Jain Malkin

typical number of rooms per physician is two to three rooms. This document also includes sample floor plans from several responding practices.

2. The annual *Cost Survey Report* includes data on total square footage and square feet per full-time-equivalent (FTE) physician. The report includes information for multispecialty practices and many individual specialties. The following table is an example of 2004 data from the 2005 *Cost Survey Report:*

Practice type	Median number of square feet per FTE physician
Multispecialty	1,950
Family practice	1,900
Pediatrics	1,619
Anesthesiology	116
Cardiology	1,959
Gastroenterology	1,374
Orthopedic surgery	2,311
Radiology	392
Urology	1,956

3. The book *Medical and Dental Space Planning: A Comprehensive Guide to Design, Equipment, and Clinical Procedures,* 3rd Edition, by Jain Malkin, provides detailed space requirements and floor plans, along with interior design and layout ideas for pleasant and efficient medical facilities.

If your facility has less square footage than the above medians, it may be time to expand your current facility or move to a new facility. If the facility is within the medians, you should evaluate the current floor plan and space utilization. There may be means of using your current space more efficiently. Are all of the exam rooms fully utilized? Does the practice offer new services that demand more room? Is the complaint related to the lack of *office* space or *clinical* space? Is renovating your current facility an option? It may be disruptive when it occurs, but it may be beneficial in the long run and doesn't require your patients to follow you to a new location.

QUESTION 11

Our schedulers believe that patients are unhappy with waiting times and delays for next-available appointments. How do we track these times and obtain benchmark numbers?

Lengthy appointment wait times can decrease patient satisfaction and deter other patients from coming to your practice. You can enlist your receptionists and schedulers to determine the current wait times. You should also include questions on the topic in your patient satisfaction survey.

Your scheduler should know or be able to calculate the next available appointment time for physical exams and follow-up appointments. To assess waiting time during an appointment, have the receptionists record the time when a patient checks in at the desk, when the nurse or medical assistant escorts the patient to the exam room, and when the patient checks out. This information can be recorded on the charge ticket or other form used during the appointment.

After you've gathered enough data, compare your numbers with benchmarks, including the following:

Average time to next appointment for new patient

Specialty	Days to appointment
Cardiology	18.8
Dermatology	24.3
OB-GYN	23.3
Orthopedic surgery	16.9

Source: Merritt, Hawkins & Associates, "Summary Report: 2004 Survey of Physician Appointment Wait Times" (Irving, TX: Merritt, Hawkins & Associates, 2004), www.merritthawkins.com (accessed October 2004).

Wait time in the medical practice

	Time in waiting room (minutes)	Time in exam room (minutes)	Total wait time (minutes)
New patient	17.4	10.5	27.9
Established patient	15.3	10.2	25.5

Source: Kelly M. Leddy, Dennis O. Kaldenberg, and Boris W. Becker, "Timeliness in Ambulatory Care Treatment: An Examination of Patient Satisfaction and Wait Times in Medical Practices and Outpatient Test and Treatment Facilities," *Journal of Ambulatory Care Management,* V. 26, No. 2, April 2003.

Leddy et al. found an inverse correlation in wait times and patient satisfaction: the longer the wait time, the lower the likelihood of recommending the practice to others and the lower overall rating of care. Patients who rated the waiting areas as very comfortable and pleasant were more tolerant of wait times than those in waiting areas rated poor for comfort.

If your group's wait times are longer than these benchmarks, then you should investigate potential causes and how to implement changes.

To decrease the wait times in your practice, consider taking one or more of the following actions:

➤ Add another physician or nonphysician provider, especially if your physicians are seeing more patients than the benchmarks (see Question #3 for benchmarks);

➤ Extend office hours to accommodate more patients per day;

➤ Hire additional staff to support the physicians;

➤ At check-in, provide patients with a form for writing down what they want to discuss with the physician in order to make the time with the physician more efficient;

- Identify opportunities to maximize patient flow and increase the number of patients seen per day;

- Encourage your staff and physicians to express their ideas for eliminating delays; and

- Modify your appointment system to schedule patients more efficiently and more accurately, or implement advanced access to offer same-day appointments (see Question #8).

It may be impossible to eliminate all delays, but practices can take steps to make wait times more tolerable – for example:

- Create a relaxing reception area with comfortable chairs, good lighting, artwork, plants, and soft music. Stock it with items to help the patients pass the time, including a variety of reading materials, games, a television, and an aquarium. Offer coffee, tea, or water. Have entertaining items available for children.

- Communicate with your patients the reasons for delays and extended wait times. Patients are more understanding about increased wait times when they know the reason for it and approximately how long it will last. Most importantly, apologize for the delay; your patients' time is also important.

Sources:

Merritt, Hawkins & Associates, "Summary Report: 2004 Survey of Physician Appointment Wait Times" (Irving, TX: Merritt, Hawkins & Associates, 2004), www.merritthawkins.com (accessed October 2004).

Kelly M. Leddy, Dennis O. Kaldenberg, and Boris W. Becker, "Timeliness in Ambulatory Care Treatment: An Examination of Patient Satisfaction and Wait Times in Medical Practices and Outpatient Test and Treatment Facilities," *Journal of Ambulatory Care Management*, V. 26, No. 2, April 2003.

Elizabeth Woodcock, *Mastering Patient Flow: More Ideas to Increase Efficiency and Earnings*, 2nd Edition (Englewood, CO: Medical Group Management Association, 2003).

QUESTION 12

How can I maximize my physicians' productivity by using the office space more efficiently?

As your medical practice searches for ways to trim costs, it is necessary to look at wasted time and motion. You do not have to build a new facility in order to improve output. One area that you can assess is physician output.

Look back through appointment schedules for the last two to three days. Divide these into half-day sessions. For each session, count how many patients the physicians saw and divide the total by the total number of hours they worked. Be careful to account for the beginning and ending clinic time, because this requires you to include overtime. Your calculation determines each session's patient-per-hour (PPH) rate, the basic yardstick showing physician output.

Finally, find the highest PPH rate of all the sessions and add a line noting it as the peak output.

Example of patient-per-hour (PPH) rates

Doctor session	Time			Patients	
	Start	Stop	Elapsed (in hrs & hundredths)	Seen	Per hour
1	9:15	12:30	3.25	12	3.69
2	9:18	12:18	3.00	15	5.00
3	8:55	11:55	3.00	16	5.33
4	9:05	12:45	3.67	10	2.72
5	8:30	12:20	3.83	11	2.87
6	12:45	3:15	2.50	13	5.20
7	12:55	3:50	2.92	14	4.79
8	1:10	5:10	4.00	10	2.50
9	1:05	4:50	3.75	18	4.80
10	1:00	4:20	3.33	15	4.50
		Average	33.25	134	4.03
		Peak			5.33

Copyright © 2002 American College of Physician Executives

Review and study the results of this report. What can the practice do to improve the number of patients seen efficiently? Why are some providers seemingly more efficient than others? What are the differences and similarities between physician sessions? Answers to these questions will help you look at your office processes and discuss potential improvements.

CHAPTER 2
Financial Management

QUESTION 13

Can you advise me on how best to manage the accounts receivable in my practice? How should I calculate A/R to compare with other practices?

You are right to be concerned about accounts receivable for your practice. Accounts receivable (A/R) is one of the key indicators of whether or not a practice is on the right financial track. The longer the accounts go uncollected, the more revenue is lost and the more the practice's expensive resources are spent on the ongoing collection effort. It is recommended that accounts receivable aging and days outstanding be included in a monthly key indicator financial report.

However, knowing your practice's A/R doesn't help without knowing how your numbers compare with the nationwide norm or with better performing practices. To compare your A/R numbers, refer to the annual MGMA *Cost Survey Report* and *Performance and Practices of Successful Medical Groups.*

MGMA uses the following definition for calculating A/R:

> **A/R** is the summation of the amounts owed to the practice by patients, third-party payers, employer groups, and others for fee-for-service (FFS) activities, with days counted from the time the invoice is submitted for payment (not date of service [DOS]).

Days in accounts receivable is calculated as:

> Total accounts receivable / [gross FFS charges (1/365)]

For example, the days in accounts receivable for primary care practices is:

> $78,718 / [$750,298 × 1/365] = 38.3 days or 1.27 months

Calculation based on per physician data.

Source: Medical Group Management Association, *Cost Survey for Multispecialty Practices: 2005 Report Based on 2004 Data* (Englewood, CO: Medical Group Management Association, 2005).

Accounts receivable figures for better performing groups

	Primary care	Medicine single specialty	Surgical single specialty
Percent of A/R > 120 days	8.48%	8.29%	8.62%
Months gross FFS charges in A/R	1.01	1.05	1.18

Note: FFS = fee for service

Source: Medical Group Management Association, *Performance and Practices of Successful Medical Groups: 2005 Report Based on 2004 Data* (Englewood, CO: Medical Group Management Association, 2005).

If your accounts receivable numbers do not compare favorably with the better performing groups studied in the MGMA report, several processes related to A/R should be investigated:

➤ Slow payers and high denial rates;

➤ Process inefficiencies in patient registration, billing, payment posting, and A/R processes;

➤ Over- or undercoding; and

➤ Inefficient use of technology tools.

The comprehensive book *Financial Management for Medical Groups: A Resource for New and Experienced Managers*, published by MGMA, provides information on calculating and managing accounts receivable.

Source:

Medical Group Management Association, *Performance and Practices of Successful Medical Groups: 2005 Report Based on 2004 Data* (Englewood, CO: Medical Group Management Association, 2005).

QUESTION 14

I would like to add another physician to meet our increasing patient demand, but the physicians are worried about the cost of bringing on another partner. How can I compare the cost vs. the benefit of bringing on a new physician?

The decision of whether or not to hire a new physician is not an easy one. The first step in your assessment is to compare the potential investment required to bring aboard a physician with the objective and subjective benefits that the physician will bring.

When calculating the expenses for your practice, include the following items:

Expenses	Estimated cost
Recruitment expenses (advertising, travel expenses, cost of recruiter, and so on)	
Physician's salary	
Benefits (health insurance, association dues, and so on)	
Physician's moving expenses covered by the practice	
Advertising and marketing expenses to promote the new physician to the public	
Malpractice insurance costs	
Additional staffing costs, if needed	
Cost of the new physician's office space and furnishings	
Cost of medical equipment and supplies the physician will use	

Revenue for new physicians is difficult to estimate and will depend on the market, the individual specialty, the physician, the time to complete licensing processes, and other factors. As a benchmark, MGMA has analyzed data related to the growth of new physicians' collections over time:

Collections, TC/NPP Excl, >=.8 FTE

	Years of experience (1 year intervals)								
	1		2		3		4		5	
	Count	Median	Count	Median	Count	Median	Count	Median	Count	Median
Medical specialists	36	$381,618	82	$523,677	58	$572,012	61	$488,225	67	$518,373
Surgical specialists	28	$584,693	58	$566,899	66	$630,815	57	$713,898	72	$614,300
Primary care	96	$252,728	201	$276,862	202	$300,814	211	$332,151	254	$328,099

Note: TC/NPP = technical component/nonphysician provider; FTE = full-time equivalent
Source: Medical Group Management Association, *Physician Compensation and Production Survey: 2006 Report Based on 2005 Data* (Englewood, CO: Medical Group Management Association, 2006).

Along with increased collections, the additional benefits of hiring an another physician include decreased patient load for current physicians, shorter appointment waiting times for patients, and decreased time on call.

Analysis of the MGMA data shows that practices subsidized the cost of new physicians until the doctors could increase production. The survey data indicate that new doctors, particularly in primary care, may need initial support, but they soon pull their own weight and contribute to the success of the practice.

Sources:

David N. Gans, "On the Edge: Pulling Their Own Weight," *MGMA Connexion*, V. 5, No. 9, October 2005.

David N. Gans, "On the Edge: What Does It Take for Physicians to Reach Peak Earnings? Time," *MGMA Connexion*, V. 2, No. 4, April 2002.

QUESTION 15

I need help in better managing our accounts payable. We have sometimes been on credit hold with vendors because of delayed payments. How can I improve the process?

Accounts payable should be monitored as closely as accounts receivable, which means calculating the accounts payable outstanding (aging) period on a monthly basis. Accounts payable should represent less than 25 percent of your average monthly expenses. To calculate the accounts payable ratio, divide the average daily purchases by the total accounts payable. If we assume that a group's total accounts payable is $50,000 and its average daily purchases are $2,805, then the accounts payable ratio is 17.82 days ($50,000/$2,805 = 17.82 days).

There are several steps you can take to improve payables management. Review your current processes on how invoices are received, approved, processed, paid, and filed. The checks should be paid on a regular schedule. You may want to start with a weekly or bimonthly schedule until the process is under control. The invoices should be filed in one location until check-writing day so that none of them are misplaced. You should take advantage of any discounts for paying within a certain time or at the time of purchase.

Also review the checking and savings account balances. Do delays occur because of inadequate funds in the checking account? Should the payment dates be adjusted to ensure adequate funds? It is helpful to project out 30 to 60 days of cash flow in order to anticipate potential timing problems.

The complete accounts payable process should be scrutinized by another employee or a physician to ensure accurate payments and limit the chance of embezzlement. This reviewer should check the source documentation, such as original receipts and purchase orders, to ensure that unauthorized or erroneous payments are not processed.

Sources:

Ernest J. Pavlock, PhD, CPA, *Financial Management for Medical Groups: A Resource for New and Experienced Managers,* 2nd Edition (Englewood, CO: Medical Group Management Association, 2000).

Darrell L. Schryver, "Question Box: Financial Ratios and Group Practice Operations," *MGM Journal,* V. 47, No. 5, September 2000.

"Watch Where Your Money Goes, Doctor," *Private Practice Success,* July 2003.

QUESTION 16

I am trying to decide if I should contract with a billing service or keep it in house. Do you have benchmarks comparing costs for outsourcing vs. in-house billing for multispecialty practices?

The decision over contracting for billing services vs. keeping them in house is a complicated one, and you, as an administrator, must carefully weigh the pros and cons.

The factors to consider for outsourcing include:

➤ The increased knowledge and experience of a company that specializes in one function, which could enhance performance and quality control;

➤ Savings for the practice in not employing and paying benefits for billing employees; and

➤ Concerns over the lack of control in not having the function in house.

Factors to consider for keeping billing within the practice include:

➤ Increased control over billing functions for quality control and compliance;

➤ Quicker implementation of changes in the billing process;

FOR MORE INFORMATION...

Billing Services

If you decide to proceed with a billing service, you might want to refer to the detailed "Billing Service Selection Checklist," available from the MGMA Website. To access this checklist, visit the Member area of the Website, www.mgma.com, and select Tools.

> Knowledge and level of experience of billing personnel and the billing function supervisor; and

> Cost of billing staff and office space compared with outsourcing.

To assess the potential costs for outsourced vs. in-house processes, gather as much data as you can. According to an MGMA *Information Exchange* (an informal questionnaire), most responding practices were charged 6 percent to 10 percent of collections by the billing services. What do the billing services in your area charge and what services do they offer?

Staff salary expenses for patient accounting staff in multi-specialty practices average 3 percent of total practice operating costs plus benefits, according to the MGMA *Cost Survey Report*. In addition to salary and benefit expenses, you should also estimate additional related costs such as building space expenses and administrative supplies.

Sources:

"Billing Services," *Information Exchange* #4840, Medical Group Management Association, July 2004.

Medical Group Management Association, *Cost Survey for Multispecialty Practices: 2005 Report Based on 2004 Data* (Englewood, CO: Medical Group Management Association, 2005).

QUESTION 17

What are the benefits of contracting with a collection agency? What percentage of accounts can they collect?

There are several reasons for practices to contract with collection agencies. The agencies charge a percentage of the amount collected relative to the potential of a total write-off. According to an *Information Exchange* (an informal survey) conducted by MGMA in September 2005, the majority of collection agencies charged 20 percent to 40 percent of the accounts. Practices may not be staffed adequately to per-

> **KEY POINT**
>
> The probability of collecting a delinquent account drops sharply with the length of delinquency. After 90 days, a business has only a 69.6 percent probability of collecting its money. By six months, the odds drop to 52.1 percent.

form intensive follow-up for aging accounts receivables, and accounts are often simply written off. Some agencies have expanded to include other services such as skip tracing and legal services.

A majority of MGMA practices contract with collection agencies. According to the 2005 *Information Exchange,* 92 percent of group practices that responded use collection agencies for past-due patient accounts. The 154 respondents differed on how long they wait before sending patients' accounts to collections. Most (54.8 percent) wait more than 120 days, while 39.7 percent wait 91 to 120 days.

Even collection agencies are not able to collect 100 percent of delinquent accounts, and the longer the practice waits to send an account to an agency, the less chance the account will be paid. A survey conducted by the Commercial Collection Agency Section of the Commercial Law League of America found that the probability of collecting a delinquent account drops sharply with the length of delinquency. After 90 days, a business has only a 69.6 percent probability of collecting its money. By six months, the odds drop to 52.1 percent.

Sources:

"Collection Agency Usage," *Information Exchange* #6483, Medical Group Management Association, September 2005.

Commercial Collection Agency Section of the Commercial Law League of America, www.ccaacollect.com.

QUESTION 18

How do I determine the fair-market value of my medical practice?

A fair-market value of a medical practice is determined by the intrinsic value of its assets, the value of its probable future income flow, and the value of its equity in the marketplace. The following factors are considered in arriving at a fair-market value:

- ➤ The economic outlook in general and the condition and outlook for the medical profession;
- ➤ The book value and the financial condition of the practice;
- ➤ The earning capacity of the practice;
- ➤ Goodwill or other intangible value;
- ➤ Sales of similar medical practices;
- ➤ Ability to retain payer contracts; and
- ➤ Ability to retain patient base and/or referral base.

Different methods of valuation consider different elements of value in arriving at an overall conclusion. Book value and adjusted book value consider the value of the practice's assets. Income methods, which include the capitalization of earnings, the capitalization of excess earnings, and the discounted future earnings, among others, concentrate on income flows as the principal determinant of value.

In addition, three basic theories constitute valuation: asset, income, and market. The asset theory bases the value of the business on the value of the business assets, whereas the income theory looks at the earnings of the business, and the market theory bases the value on comparable sales of similar businesses.

With the asset theory, four methods of valuation are frequently considered: book value, fair-market value of assets, liquidation value, and cost to create. Two methodologies are employed in assessing the value based on income: the capitalization of earnings and the capitalization of excess earnings.

Source:

Darrell L. Schryver, DPA, "Question Box: How to Determine Fair Market Value," *MGM Journal*, V. 45, No. 6, November 1998.

QUESTION

I will be starting my own practice soon, and I'm wondering how soon the practice will make a profit. What are the typical start-up costs? Do you have benchmarks for profit and loss for a medical practice over the first few years?

Estimates for start-up costs for a small primary care practice range from $60,000 to $100,000, depending on the location and your purchasing decisions. Specialty practices may have higher costs, depending on equipment and supplies that are needed. You can spend $50,000 to $65,000 on just furniture, medical equipment, telephones, and information technology. The costs for the practice management systems (for billing and collections) vary from $10,000 to $25,000 unless these functions are outsourced. Purchasing an electronic health record system at the beginning will eliminate the need to convert the system at a later date, but this will add to your total costs.

You also need to consider the number and types of employees that you hire, as well as their salary and benefit expenses. You will need a minimum of 2.5 full-time-equivalent employees; however, 4 to 4.5 employees are recommended. Sources for employee salaries are listed in the table on page 43. Remember to add the practice's obligations for workers' compensation, Social Security, retirement packages, and related expenses to the total expenses.

Revenue for new starting physicians is difficult to estimate and will depend on the market, the physician, the time to complete licensing processes, and other factors. As a benchmark, MGMA has analyzed data related to the growth of new physicians' collections in group practices:

Collections, TC/NPP Excl, >=.8 FTE

	Years of experience (1 year intervals)									
	1		2		3		4		5	
	Count	Median	Count	Median	Count	Median	Count	Median	Count	Median
Medical specialists	36	$381,618	82	$523,677	58	$572,012	61	$488,225	67	$518,373
Surgical specialists	28	$584,693	58	$566,899	66	$630,815	57	$713,898	72	$614,300
Primary care	96	$252,728	201	$276,862	202	$300,814	211	$332,151	254	$328,099

Note: TC/NPP = technical component/nonphysician provider; FTE = full-time equivalent
Source: Medical Group Management Association, *Physician Compensation and Production Survey: 2006 Report Based on 2005 Data* (Englewood, CO: Medical Group Management Association, 2006).

Compensation for a solo practitioner is what is left after expenses. As a starting physician, you may have to lower your salary expectations in the first year or two to cover practice expenses and loan payments.

The number of patient visits and growth of patient visits in your new practice will depend on market demand, success of your advertising efforts, ability to obtain referrals, and so on. Some practices may receive enough new patients to reach capacity in 6 to 12 months, while others, especially primary care practices, may take 18 to 24 months. Depending on expenses, patient demand, and other factors, you are probably looking at 6 to 12 months, or even longer, until your gross practice income exceeds your monthly expenses.

Checklist for New Practice Start-Up

Tools to improve your group practice from the MGMA Health Care Consulting Group.

By Daniel P. Stech, MBA, Darrell L. Schryver, DPA, and Bruce A. Johnson, JD, MPA

Medical Group Management Association

This document is intended for physicians starting a new practice. The document is only a reference tool and should not be considered comprehensive. Your local market conditions, specific laws and regulations in your state, and other factors may influence the start-up process. Consultants from the MGMA Health Care Consulting Group, with extensive experience in medical practice development, operations, and management, are available to assist you with this process. MGMA also has a wealth of other resources that can be helpful. For more information, please contact us toll-free at 877.ASK.MGMA (275.6462), ext. 877, or e-mail consulting@mgma.com.

Objective: Business and Financial Planning			
Successful practices begin with a plan that describes the strategic goals for the organization, its financial and other resource needs. Capital partners such as banks may require a formal business plan before approving credit.			
Strategies: Strategic plan	A strategic plan is your road map to the future. The plan should identify the goals for your practice and how you intend to achieve those goals. A strategic plan should also recognize issues in your market that will benefit or hinder your success.		
	Tasks:	Mission, vision and values	
		Goals and action plans	
		Market analysis	
		Marketing plan development	

Strategies: Budget	The value of an operating budget for your practice cannot be overstated. A budget is your first tool in measuring practice performance, understanding your sources of revenue, practice expenses and capital needs. Two general types of budgets may be required: (1) a start-up budget (relating to consulting, legal, accounting, and other start-up costs), and (2) an operating budget to project revenue and expenses once the practice is operating. The budgeting process should also consider cash flow issues associated with high and low patient volumes due to practice growth, credentialing requirements and payment delays, as well as sources of operating capital during low cash periods. All initial budgets should be informed and continually adjusted based on your decisions related to practice operations and other matters.
	Tasks: Start-up budget
	Pro forma projections
	Capital needs
	Income/Revenue
	Overhead/Expense

Objective: Operations

The focus on medical practice operations must be multifaceted to encompass all of the activities and resources required to operate and manage medical practices. Operational issues associated with new practice development range from the development of a solid legal structure for the practice, to developing financial management systems, finding a place to practice, and hiring staff. Most established practices tend to organize and manage these resources internally, but many new practices find that certain functions such as billing and benefits administration may also be effectively outsourced.

Strategies: Legal	A qualified health care attorney can be an invaluable resource in today's health care environment.	
	Tasks:	Health care attorney
		Form of entity (i.e., professional corporation, professional LLC)
		Organizational formation (i.e., articles of incorporation)
		Governance, buy/sell and employment issues
		Tax identification number
		Medicare provider number
Strategies: Finance	Once the decision to develop a practice has been made, a qualified CPA should be selected to provide guidance on tax and financial management issues including the practice's financial chart of accounts. Although physicians finishing residency commonly have debt, starting a new practice from scratch will likely require more debt. Evaluate different banks in your community to find which ones specialize in lending to medical practices.	
	Tasks:	Accountant
		Capital/Credit/Banking
		Chart of accounts
		Fee schedule development
Strategies: Insurance	In many cases, the same liability carrier providing malpractice coverage will also offer corporate/general liability and other forms of insurance coverage. Consult your leases and other contracts to assure you're obtaining the type of insurance that's required under these arrangements. Shop around for insurance before you buy and consider group-purchasing opportunities as a means to conserve costs.	
	Tasks:	Malpractice
		Corporate
		Health and disability
		Life (Personal)

Strategies: Credentialing/ Third-party payors	Contracts are the lifeblood of most medical practices because they provide access to patients. Even the most skilled physician needs to be credentialed with hospitals, health plans and other organizations, and credentialing is a prerequisite for physicians to be paid for their services by third-party payors. Credentialing can take many months in some instances, so getting started sooner rather than later is always advisable. Evaluating contract terms and reimbursement levels is a daunting task. This element of your new practice requires organization and attention to detail.	
	Tasks: Credentialing	
	Contracts: Health plans, HMOs, and PPOs	
	Hospital privileges	
Strategies: Facilities	Facilities encompass everything from actual building space to the equipment and supplies needed to practice medicine. It is generally more cost effective to use existing clinic space rather than building out new. Physicians starting a new practice can commonly access space being vacated by a retiring physician or rent space in an established medical office building as a means to conserve cost and enhance access to patients. Check with hospital administrators or commercial realtors to learn more.	
	Tasks: Space needs	
	Identification of facility	
	Lease agreement	
	Equipment and supplies	
	Information/Billing systems	
	Utilities	

Strategies: Staffing	Staffing is a critical success factor in any new business. Your practice needs the right people and the right number of people to support it. Staffing also represents a significant expense. Some physicians may be inclined to skimp on staffing to save costs – they usually regret it. Staff can be added over time, but a physician needs to determine what is appropriate for startup. Some functions may be purchased or outsourced from a hospital, MSO, or billing company.	
	Tasks:	Office management/administration
		Reception/scheduling
		Clinical: Nurse/MA
		Insurance/Billing
		Personnel policies
		Benefits
Strategies: Other	There are numerous tasks associated with a practice start-up and this list just brushes the surface. Always consider your options because wrong decisions can be costly. Form relationships with established physicians and use them as mentors. Managing a physician practice gets more complex each day. Having good information is essential and MGMA is the source of practice management information. Also, get to know professional practice administrators in your area. They'll be well positioned to help you answer some questions related to the management of your practice.	
	Tasks:	Networking/Referral relationships
		Mentors and information sources
		IPA/Contracting network membership
		Marketing activities
		MGMA membership

© 2002 Medical Group Management Association. All rights reserved.

Sources:

David N. Gans, "On the Edge: What Does It Take for Physicians to Reach Peak Earnings? Time," *MGMA Connexion*, V. 2, No. 4, April 2002.

Gail Levy, "Starting a Practice," *Family Practice Management*, V. 8, No. 1, January 2001.

Ken Terry, "Going Solo: Start-up Basics," *Medical Economics*, V. 80, No. 114, May 9, 2003.

QUESTION 20

I am trying to evaluate the pros and cons of a centralized vs. decentralized billing office. What are your thoughts?

Many practices and other businesses prefer centralized billing offices, believing that economies of scale will lower overall costs compared to having several separate offices. Other benefits of centralization include:

➤ Standardization of processes, data collection, and reports;

➤ Development of expertise with the increase of employee specialization;

➤ Sharing of knowledge within one office;

➤ Improved patient relations with one location offering answers to all billing questions; and

➤ Cross coverage when needed.

There are disadvantages to centralized billing offices. The process may suffer due to decreased interaction between billers and providers, which is important in the specialty practices, such as oncology, with complex billing issues. As the billing office grows in size, the complexity may affect economies of scale. Larger information systems may be needed, costing more, and employees may feel trapped in a limiting system of specialization.

Elizabeth Woodcock, MBA, FACMPE, and Loc Nguyen compared the operating costs and collections of practices with centralized billing offices with those of decentralized ones (see table on next page). Those with centralized operations had lower business office expenses than those without. However, collections took longer in centralized offices, and the collection percentages were mixed. Their conclusion was that a hybrid centralized / decentralized billing office may be best, "allowing the practice to capture the economies that are possible while retaining the relationships, communication, productivity, and control that are essential to success."

Comparison between decentralized and centralized billing offices

	Decentralized	Centralized
Business office expenses (median per physician)		
Single specialties	$22,571	$17,455
Multispecialties	$19,962	$16,873
Collection percentage		
Single specialties	96.02%	97.59%
Multispecialties	98.50%	97.56%
A/R days outstanding		
Single specialties	56.0	57.5
Multispecialties	52.8	57.4

Source: Elizabeth W. Woodcock and Loc Nguyen, "The Economics of Central Billing Offices," *MGM Journal*, V. 47, No. 3, May 2000.

Whichever model you choose, remember that all billing offices, whether centralized or decentralized, require clear procedures, quality control, and appropriate performance goals to be successful.

A CLOSER LOOK . . .

Fact box

Better performing groups	
Centralized billing	69.11%
Decentralized	9.76%
Hybrid	21.11%

Source: Medical Group Management Association, *Performance and Practices of Successful Medical Groups: 2005 Report Based on 2004 Data* (Englewood, CO: Medical Group Management Association, 2005).

QUESTION 21

What is the best method of measuring the productivity of my billing office? Are there benchmarks for productivity of collectors, charge posters, payment posters, and so on?

Comparative staff productivity data are difficult to locate and should be used wisely. Each practice is unique in terms of payer mix, staff mix, and business office functions. Therefore, staff productivity will vary. You should also benchmark your practice with MGMA survey data to compare the number of business office staff and expenses, gross charges, accounts receivable data, and other financial data. If you are within medical practice norms, your staff productivity may be acceptable.

Medical practice experts Deborah Walker Keegan, PhD, FACMPE, Sara M. Larch, MSHA, FACMPE, and Elizabeth W. Woodcock, MBA, FACMPE, CPC, provide the following figures for staff workload ranges. They recommend that you review and emphasize the quality of the work, not just the quantity. The ranges are based on seven hours per day, assuming one hour for breaks and interruptions.

Staff activity	Per day	Per hour
Charge entry encounters (without registration)	375–525	55–75
Transactions posted manually	525–875	75–125
Account follow-up research correspondence and resolve by phone	n/a	6–12
Self-pay follow-up	70–90	10–13
Patient billing inquiries	125–140	15–18

© 2004 Walker, Larch, Woodcock.

Note: Workload may depend upon your information systems, Internet access, facility, flow of work (e.g., documentation required), additional tasks assigned, specialty(ies), and other variables.

Source: Deborah L. Walker, MBA, FACMPE, Sara M. Larch, MSHA, FACMPE, and Elizabeth W. Woodcock, MBA, FACMPE, CPC, *The Physician Billing Process: Avoiding Potholes in the Road to Getting Paid,* p. 158 (Englewood, CO: Medical Group Management Association, 2004).

If the billing staff workload is below the above ranges and your practice financial ratios are below MGMA benchmarks, you should investigate possible reasons and ways of correcting the issue:

> Are you using the practice management system to its full capabilities? Have staff members received adequate training, and are they using the program with maximum effectiveness? You may want to work with the system vendor to identify additional efficiencies.

> Ask assistance from business office employees in identifying ways of increasing the department productivity. Can they identify issues that impede their productivity?

> Develop an incentive program based on increasing the group's billing efficiency and financial ratios. Make the employees vested in increased productivity, lowered accounts receivable, fewer patient complaints about bills, and so on.

QUESTION 22

I have been hired as an administrator of a new practice. How do I develop the fee schedule for the practice's services?

The Medicare physician fee schedule can be used as a basis for developing your practice's fee schedule. The schedule, based on the resource-based relative value scale (RBRVS), is published annually in the Federal Register or is available online at the Centers for Medicare & Medicaid Services Website: www.cms.hhs.gov/physicianfeesched.

Many administrators then set their fees at a certain percentage above the Medicare schedule or adjust the schedule based on types of services provided. The RBRVS tends to place relatively higher value on the evaluation and management (E & M) services, giving lower values to procedures.

FOR MORE INFORMATION...

There are many consultants and businesses that provide information on average fees or will consult with you to develop a fair fee schedule for your practice and location. The following are a few contacts:

Contact	Website	Telephone
Ingenix	Ingenix.com	800.464.3649
MagMutual Healthcare Solutions	Coderscentral.com	800.253.4945
Practice Management Information Corporation	PMIConline.com	800.med.shop
EMC Corporation (Captiva)	Captivasoftware.com	858.320.1000
MGMA Healthcare Consulting Group	MGMA.com	888.275.6462

If your group performs many surgical procedures, you may want to use another system or set a higher conversion factor for surgical services.

After your practice has been in operation for several months, you should review the fee schedule. Compare your charges with the reimbursement you have been receiving from insurance companies. Most payer contracts will pay the lesser of the fee charged or the contract rate. You may want to increase your charges if you've been receiving full reimbursement from any payers; your charges should be above their reimbursement rate to ensure that you are receiving the maximum allowable.

After you've been in operation for a sufficient time, you will want to analyze your costs to ensure your charges are greater than the costs of providing services. Determining your cost per relative value unit (RVU) will help you determine your costs per Current Procedural Terminology (CPT) code. You may want to revise your fee schedule over time to a cost-based fee schedule. MGMA has several articles on using RVUs for cost analysis and a book, *RVUs: Applications for Medical Practice Success,* by Kathryn Glass.

Whatever method you use to set your fee schedule, review it on a regular basis, annually or biannually, to ensure that it reflects changing costs and reimbursements.

What are the best financial ratios and reports I should use to monitor the financial health of my practice?

There are almost as many opinions on what the key performance indicators are for medical practices as there are indicators. Also, there are key performance indicators that need to be monitored on a monthly basis, while others are part of the year-end report and review.

Rosemarie Nelson, MS, MGMA Health Care Consulting Group, recommends monitoring the following indicators on a monthly basis to ensure the financial health of your practice:

> ➤ **Trends in gross charges** – Have charges declined, increased, or remained the same? Is there anything out of the ordinary? Are all charges posted?

> ➤ **Accounts receivable (A/R)** – How many days of gross fee-for-service charges are outstanding in A/R? What percentage of total A/R is more than 90 and 120 days old? Compare your organization to similar practices in MGMA's *Cost Survey Report,* and then compare your benchmark to those of better-performing practices in MGMA's *Performance and Practices of Successful Medical Groups.*

> ➤ **Date of service** – Is the cycle time from date of service (DOS) to claim submission reasonable based on

established standards in your practice? For example, make a point to post all outpatient visits or charges within 24 hours of DOS and all charges for inpatient visits within 72 hours of DOS. Review variances from these standards.

➤ **Operating costs** – Look at costs as a percentage of medical revenue, which can provide insight to efficient operations. Compare your costs with MGMA's survey reports.

➤ **Your group's needs** – What key issue does the practice face? Is it staff turnover, physician recruitment, the development of a new lab, or the opening of a satellite clinic? How can these issues be addressed?

A survey of medical groups identified by MGMA as better performers in profitability and cost management typically generate the following reports monthly and annually to evaluate financial performance:

➤ **Financial reports:**
  ➢ Accounts receivable aging report;
  ➢ Cost reports by department, provider, and location;
  ➢ Income statement;
  ➢ Balance sheet; and
  ➢ Statement of cash flow.

➤ **Practice management reports:**
  ➢ Collections system summary analysis;
  ➢ Untracked encounter forms report;
  ➢ Unbilled revenue report;
  ➢ Billing summary;
  ➢ Procedures analysis; and

➤ Managed care plan profitability (capitation analysis).

Olga Quintana and Cesar Ortiz present seven key indicator reports for medical practices in their *MGMA Connexion* article. The seven key indicators are:

➤ Current capacity and capability of each provider or business unit, including ratio of new vs. established patients and appointment wait time;

➤ Actual weekly charges per provider and business unit, because a monthly report may be too late if charges change rapidly;

➤ Payer mix for the practice, each provider, or each business unit. This report ensures a well-balanced portfolio of payer categories and provides a baseline for plan-marketing efforts;

➤ Collections and collection rate for each provider and business unit;

➤ Trended value of A/R for the medical practice, broken out by payer category;

➤ Monthly costs by provider and business unit; and

➤ Actual vs. budgeted net balance per provider and business unit. Reporting net revenue will show providers the effect that costs have on profit.

Nonfinancial indicators must also be included in regular analyses of practice performance. Chapter 1 also discusses some of these indicators and tools.

Sources:

Rosemarie Nelson, "Q & A: Maintain Financial Health with a Monthly Checkup," *MGMA e-Connexion,* Issue 31, May 2003.

Bob Redling, "Size Matters: Financial Management Traps: Many Groups Fail at Internal Controls, Financial Audits," *MGMA Connexion,* V. 2, No. 9, October 2002.

Cesar A. Ortiz and Olga Quintana, "Buckling Down to Business: Seven Key Indicator Reports for Medical Practices," *MGMA Connexion,* V. 2, No. 9, October 2002.

QUESTION 24

I'm reviewing the operations for my cardiology practice, but I don't know how my practice compares with others. For example, what are the typical overhead expenses for medical practices?

MGMA has two excellent reports for comparing the financial and operation ratios of medical practices. The annual *Cost Survey Report* provides detailed practice data. The *Performance and Practices of Successful Medical Groups* report analyzes the data and operations of practices identified as better performers to provide a higher benchmarking standard.

To ensure you're comparing apples to apples, the definition of operating costs/overhead for the MGMA reports is:

Operating costs/overhead: The cost of the practice's support staff, information technology, medical and surgical supplies, building and occupancy, furniture and equipment, administrative supplies and services, professional liability insurance premiums, other insurance premiums, outside professional fees, promotion and marketing, clinical laboratory, radiology and imaging, other ancillary services, and fees paid to contracting services. Physician and other providers' salaries and benefits are *not* included.

Operating cost data for medical group practices identified as better performing groups

	Primary care	Medicine single specialty	Surgical single specialty
Total operating cost as a percentage of total medical revenue	55.14%	45.08%	41.38%
Total operating cost per FTE physician	$333,339	$526,237	$489,416

Note: FTE = Full-time-equivalent

Source: Medical Group Management Association, *Performance and Practices of Successful Medical Groups: 2005 Report Based on 2004 Data* (Englewood, CO: Medical Group Management Association, 2005).

Remember to look at more than just the overhead. It's not necessarily a problem if your group's overhead is high compared with industry norms. Some medical groups identified as MGMA better performers have very productive physicians with high overhead ratios. This may indicate that nurse practitioners or physician assistants are used to expand productivity or that ancillary services are provided in these practices. It is okay if your overhead is high if the net income is high as well.

The MGMA *Chart of Accounts for Health Care Organizations* provides an accounting system for tracking operating costs in a format compatible with the MGMA *Cost Survey Report* and *Successful Medical Groups* report.

Sources:

Medical Group Management Association, *Performance and Practices of Successful Medical Groups: 2005 Report Based on 2004 Data* (Englewood, CO: Medical Group Management Association, 2005).

Center for Research in Ambulatory Healthcare Administration/Medical Group Management Association, *Chart of Accounts for Health Care Organizations* (Englewood, CO: Medical Group Management Association, 1998).

QUESTION  25

I would like to get the bad debt for my orthopedic practice under control. How can we manage our bad debt to ensure it is not out of line with the industry average? What is the benchmark for bad debt for surgical practices?

Remember, there are two kinds of bad debt: (1) bad debt from commercial payers (health insurance, for example) and self-pay patients, and (2) contractual write-offs and denied claims by payers (denials are discussed in Question #28). The MGMA benchmarks for the first type of bad debt for group practices are shown here.

Bad debts due to FFS activities per FTE physician

Primary care		Medicine specialties		Surgical specialties	
Better performers	All respondents	Better performers	All respondents	Better performers	All respondents
$1,542	$5,709	$11,683	$26,085	$9,957	$21,298

Source: Medical Group Management Association, *Performance and Practices of Successful Medical Groups: 2005 Report Based on 2004 Data* (Englewood, CO: Medical Group Management Association, 2005).

If your practice is experiencing higher bad debt than the benchmarks, you will need to identify the source of the problem and then identify solutions. To identify the source, you will need to review several operational issues and financial ratios.

Start by analyzing the bad debt and your accounts receivable (A/R). Is the chief culprit self-pay patients or payers? Is there one payer that leads the pack for denying payments? (See Question #13 for help with A/R.) If the bad debt is related to payers, what are the reasons for the lack of payment? Review the contract, claims completion and submission processes, reasons for denials and rejections, and so on. If bad debt is largely caused by self-pay patients, is it related to inaccurate patient information or inadequate steps to ensure payment, including obtaining commitment to pay at time of service?

Bad debt may be caused by little or no follow-up to claims, whether or not the payer is a managed care company or patient. What processes are in place if a claim is denied, rejected, or otherwise not paid within a designated period? Are there adequate personnel to follow up on claims, and do they have the training and resources needed to complete the process? If there are insufficient resources for adequate follow-up, should outstanding accounts be turned over to collection agencies that have knowledgeable staff committed to collections? (Question #17 provides advice related to the use of collection agencies.)

It is possible to turn around an area of concern such as high bad debt. Michael Schaffer worked with another orthopedics practice to complete a successful turnaround of its financial picture. He used several measures to bring about the turnaround, including the following:

- ➤ Understanding the problems;

- ➤ Creating physician and staff buy-in;

- ➤ Developing goals (e.g., achieving the MGMA benchmark for bad debt);

- ➤ Building new processes and the infrastructure to support them; and

- ➤ Ensuring adequate training and knowledge to successfully complete the processes.

Once changes are implemented, it is important to continue monitoring the financial ratios, like bad debt, compared with the developed goals. If the goals aren't being attained, it may be necessary to identify the obstacles to achieving success and modify the processes.

Source:

Michael Schaffer, "Six Months to Improved Cash Flow and Productivity," *MGMA Connexion*, V. 2, No. 6, July 2002.

Where can I find productivity standards for coders, that is, the number of charts per hour or charts per day?

As with billing office productivity, coding productivity should be used wisely, with the understanding that each practice has a different payer mix, different staff numbers and mix, and different responsibilities for its coders. An article from the American Health Information Management Association (www.ahima.org) provided productivity standards for coders in hospitals and physician practices. The following productivity expectations were for coders who did not have multiple responsibilities:

Record type	Expectation per day
Clinic and physician office visits	108
Ambulatory surgery records	30
Minor procedures	44
Outpatient tests (lab, radiology, and so on)	230
ER visits	106

Source: Rose T. Dunn and Christina Mainord, "The Latest Look at Coding Trends," *Journal of AHIMA*, V. 72, No. 7, July/August 2001.

Copyright © 2001 American Health Information Management Association. Reprinted with permission.

Who is responsible for setting the CPT and diagnosis codes – the physician or the coder?

This question is very controversial. Some coders believe that only they have the requisite education and expertise to do this – not the physician – and thus should be held responsible for setting the codes. It is important to note that some physicians actually agree with this premise.

However, the physician is ultimately responsible for choosing which code to use, so physicians are best advised to either work in direct concert with the coder or code the services keeping in mind the coder's advice and/or direction. Regardless of how the service is coded or who codes it, the physician is ultimately responsible.

Notably, many consultants recommend that administrators require their physicians to personally code every service and procedure, but you will not find agreement with this school of thought in the billing/coding industry.

QUESTION 28

My practice is suffering from an increasing number of claims rejected by payers. Do you know what the average is for percentage of claims denied? What can I do to reverse this trend?

The ideal is to have claim denials at 5 percent or less of total claims submitted. Better performing groups in the MGMA *Performance and Practices of Successful Medical Groups: 2005 Report Based on 2004 Data* typically had 5 percent of claims denied on the first submission.

There are eight major reasons for denials:

➤ Patient registration errors;

➤ Lack of insurance verification;

➤ Invalid ICD-9 code at the time of charge entry;

➤ Incomplete information relating to referrals and preauthorizations;

➤ Duplicate bills for the same services;

➤ Medical necessity – correctly linking the ICD-9 and the CPT codes;

➤ Complete documentation for the medical services provided; and

➤ Bundled or noncovered services – correctly using modifiers or editing systems.

Analyze the source of the denials to identify the top reasons in your practice. You may be able to determine if the problem is related to one or two payers or processes. If the denials are related to in-house issues, you should review the processes involved with patient registration, including insurance verification, coding, documentation, and referrals. How should they be improved? How can errors be reduced or eliminated?

Denied claims should be adjusted based on the reason for the denial and then resubmitted. When resubmitting the claim, include a letter to the payer explaining the reason for the second submission. Identify the claim and include supporting documents to help support the claim, providing information or data not included the first time.

If one or two payers continue to be an issue, continue to follow up by meeting with the payer's representative, contacting individuals higher in the organization, working with your attorney, and, ultimately, deciding if there is sufficient reason to end the contract with the payer.

Sources:

Sara Larch, MS, FACMPE, and Deborah L. Walker, MBA, FACMPE, "Improve Your Revenue Cycle: Five Key Steps," MGMA Annual Meeting Presentation, October 2004.

Sara M. Larch and Brian T. Smith, "Improving the Revenue Stream of Your Faculty Practice Plan: Charge Rejection and Accounts Receivable Management," *APA Matrix*, V. 16, No. 2, 2001.

The practice board and I are struggling with how to deal with uninsured patients in our practice. Are there any guidelines that would help us develop a policy for discounting services for the uninsured or cash-paying patients?

Practice administrators typically have two main concerns when dealing with uninsured patients: compliance with Medicare regulations and collecting some payment for the services provided.

The Department of Health and Human Services (HHS) Office of Inspector General (OIG) and the Centers for Medicare & Medicaid Services (CMS) released a guide on Feb. 19, 2004, addressing concerns about the provision of discount or charity care to the uninsured and underinsured.

The guide stated that federal law does not prohibit Medicare providers from offering discounts to the uninsured.

However, the government dislikes waiver and discount policies that fail to determine a patient's financial need. An OIG Special Fraud Alert issued in 1991 noted that it is not enough for a group practice to have a form for needy patients to fill out. Instead, the practice must make a good-faith effort to verify that a patient is indeed financially needy. This could include requesting the patient's latest tax return and last pay stub.

For federal health care program beneficiaries who do not demonstrate financial need, providers must make a good-faith effort to collect coinsurance amounts. This should include notifying patients of their obligations and giving them an appropriate amount of time to reimburse the practice for these services. After completing this process, group practices may write off these bad debts.

To limit write-offs, you can put in place several steps to increase collections from self-pay patients:

➤ Have a specific credit policy informing patients when they will be expected to pay;

➤ Send the initial invoice quickly, with follow-up statements at regular and frequent intervals;

➤ Use "address service requested" forms in case patients move;

➤ Train your employees on understanding your credit policies and how to work with patients with outstanding accounts; and

➤ For patients who aren't paying because they feel the bill is in error, explain the bill and correct it if there are any errors.

For patients with a true financial need, practice administrators should also contact state and county public health agencies or health advocacy organizations for assistance. Health advocacy organizations may have or know of benefit programs that assist patients in paying for health services or provide benefits counseling. Local public health agencies may be good resources for practices in developing sliding-scale fee programs for uninsured and underinsured patients.

A sliding-scale fee program should not be a predetermined separate fee schedule for self-pay patients. It is better to bill at full charge and then determine appropriate discounts or payment programs on a patient-by-patient basis, based on need. See Question #25 for additional information on handling bad debt.

Sources:

MGMA Government Affairs Department Washington Link, "The Impact of Recent OIG Guidance on Patient Discounts," *MGMA Connexion*, V. 4, No. 4, April 2004.

Tracy Spears, "Know-How: Out of Their Pockets: 10 Ways to Improve Collections from Self-pay Patients," *MGMA Connexion*, V. 5, No. 10, November 2005.

Bob Redling, "Know-How: Helping the Uninsured: No Need to Go It Alone," *MGMA Connexion*, V. 2, No. 3, March 2002.

"Party Line: Different Fee Schedules for Self-pay Patients?" *MGMA Connexion*, V. 4, No. 10, November 2004.

What steps can I take to improve collections from patients with high deductibles?

With the expected growth in health savings accounts (HSAs) and other high-deductible health plans, practices will need to modify operations to ensure maximum reimbursement. There are several steps you can take to prepare for working with these patients and their insurance plans:

➤ **Patient education** – Patients previously covered by managed care plans may not understand their responsibilities with the new coverage. Front desk employees should review the plan's coverage and

A CLOSER LOOK...

MGMA distributed an *Information Exchange* (an informal survey) asking members about their processes in dealing with HSA or health reimbursement arrangement (HRA) covered patients. When asked how the practices collect from these patients:

- ✔ 79.5 percent attempt to collect the copayment at the time of visit;
- ✔ 38.4 percent attempt to collect the coinsurance at the visit;
- ✔ 24.7 percent attempt to collect the estimated cost of the visit; and
- ✔ 16.4 percent collect nothing from the patient at the time of visit and bill the insurance carrier.

Of patients with HSA or HRA insurance:

- ✔ 38.3 percent have payment care options; and
- ✔ 61.7 percent do not have payment care options.

---

the patient's deductible at the time of registration, explaining to the patient the process for billing and payment.

➤ **Collection at time of service** – Patients covered by HSAs typically don't have copayments. The plans vary on expecting the patient to pay at time of service or waiting for a claim to be processed by the insurance plan. However, you may want to obtain credit card information to be able to charge the card after a period of nonpayment.

➤ **Billing and collections** – High-deductible plans have several different methods for reimbursing patients or practices, either by reimbursing the health care provider, paying the patient when receipts are submitted, or providing the patient a debit card to make payments. Understanding the payment process at the time of registration will set expectations for both the patient and the practice.

As with all patients and payers, it is important for you to ensure that complete and accurate patient information is obtained during registration, claims are submitted with full information, and adequate follow-up is applied to all claims.

Collections from HSA patients may also be affected because of patients delaying or avoiding visits to health care providers. An early study by Definity Health, a Minneapolis-based provider of consumer-driven health plans, showed an 11 percent decrease in health care utilization for consumers with HSAs and similar plans. You may address this challenge by educating patients on the importance of preventive health services and early detection of health issues. Sending out reminders for annual physical exams and visit follow-ups may help maintain visit numbers, especially with HSA plans that cover preventive exams.

> **KEY POINT**
>
> As with all patients and payers, it is important to ensure that complete and accurate patient information is obtained during registration, claims are submitted with full information, and adequate follow-up is applied to all claims.

Sources:

Debbie Welle-Powell, "HSAs – Friends or Foes?" *MGMA Connexion*, V. 6, No. 2, February 2006.

Susan B. Childs, "Health Savings Accounts (HSAs), Healthcare Reimbursement Accounts (HRAs) and Other High Deductible Health Plans (HDHPs): How They Affect Patient Behavior and Healthcare Administration's Response," ACMPE Paper, August 2005.

"High-Deductible Health Insurance Plans – HSAs and HRAs," *Information Exchange* #6484, Medical Group Management Association, September 2005.

QUESTION 31

I've heard of a trend toward hospitals compensating physicians for emergency room call coverage. What information is available about this issue?

Hobart Collins, CMPE, MGMA Health Care Consulting Group principal, offers the following information:

Pay for taking hospital emergency room (ER) calls is a hot topic for specialists in many parts of the country. A survey conducted by the American College of Physician Executives in 2005 found that 46.6 percent of respondents' hospitals paid specialists to take ER calls. While 44.5 percent of those responding currently were not paying specialists for taking ER calls, 46.4 percent of that group reported that they had considered the matter recently.*

Historically, most physicians have voluntarily taken calls at hospital ERs for reasons that included medical staff bylaw requirements, a sense of professional or ethical obligation, or civic commitment. Today, however, most specialists expect to receive some form of remuneration for taking ER calls.

The desire of a specialist, or group of specialists, to receive such a stipend obviously must coincide with a hospital's willingness to pay – and this leads to the key question of the fair market value, or reasonableness, of a specific compensation level. The specialist wants as much money as s/he can get, and the hospital probably wants to pay as little as possible; this is a typical starting point in negotiating price. Such transactions are readily resolved in the commercial world, where fair market value generally is defined as the price agreed to by a willing buyer and a willing seller.

In contrast, negotiations over price in the health care environment are complicated by regulatory, compliance,

---

* American College of Physician Executives, "On-call Survey: Physician Leaders Distressed by Specialist Shortage; On Call Pay Controversial," ACMPE.org, www.acpe.org/Articles/MayJune_05/Steiger.pdf (accessed July 29, 2006).

and legal considerations relating to fair market value or "reasonableness." Both parties must be aware of these considerations and establish a contractual arrangement that satisfies both economic and regulatory aspects. Compliance and regulatory issues are of equal concern to both parties: the specialists and the hospital. Certainly everyone will want an agreement concerning pay for specialist ER calls to be satisfactory to legal counsel.

Goals for payment arrangements

Objective criteria for establishing specialist remuneration for ER calls include consideration of:

- Market-based compensation for specialists;

- Specific time commitments of ER calls;

- Restrictions the call obligations may impose (for example, the specialist's time on call must be exclusively dedicated to the ER);

- Historic frequency of active engagement of the specialist in the ER caring for patients vs. availability in "stand-by" mode (in other words, the frequency with which the specialist is actually called to the ER);

- Potential private-practice income forfeitures for specialists taking ER calls;

- How the cost of the stipend arrangement with voluntary specialists compares to the cost if the hospital employed an adequate number of specialists to provide the same service. For a 24-hours-a-day, seven-days-a-week, 365-days-a-year exclusive service, this would require roughly five full-time physicians per specialty; and

- Market comparables, i.e., what similar organizations in similar markets pay for similar commitments.

A CLOSER LOOK...

On-call specialist daily stipends, 2005

ENT	$250 to $500
General surgeons	$300 to $600
Neurologists	$100 to $400
Neurosurgeons	$400 to $1,200
Obstetricians	$275 to $500
Orthopedists	$350 to $800
Urologists	$50 to $350

Figures are estimates based on helping more than 100 hospitals develop call coverage stipends.

Copyright © HealthCare Appraisers, Inc.

Source: HealthCare Appraisers, Inc., Del Ray Beach, FL (www.healthcareappraisers.com).

What is reasonable payment?

There are no standardized formulas for determining reasonable payment. A prime compliance consideration in determining fair-market-value compensation for specialists who participate in ER calls is *Federal Regulation* § 53.4958-6: "Rebuttable presumption that a transaction is not an excess benefit transaction."[†] It states that payments under a compensation arrangement are presumed to be reasonable if the following conditions are satisfied:

➤ "The compensation arrangement or the terms of the property transfer are approved in advance by an authorized body of the applicable tax-exempt organization ... composed entirely of individuals who do not have a conflict of interest ... with respect to the compensation arrangement;

---

† "Rebuttable presumption that a transaction is not an excess benefit transaction." 2006 Federal Register, §53.4958-6, www.access.gpo.gov/nara/cfr/waisidx_04/26cfr53_04.htm. P34,252L.

➤ "The authorized body obtained and relied upon appropriate data as to comparability prior to making its determinations ..."; and

➤ "The authorized body adequately documented the basis for its determination."[‡]

Although these considerations obviously relate directly to the hospital and its decision-making process, they should interest the specialist seeking pay for ER calls for two reasons: First, the prudent hospital is not going to agree to arrangements that run contrary to the regulatory requirements, and, second, there may be financial penalties to both parties participating in an excess benefit transaction. There has been discussion in Washington, D.C., that the regulations might be amended to jeopardize a hospital's tax-exempt status in the event of an excess-benefit transaction.

Most organizations that are confronting specialist pay for ER calls seek an independent, outside opinion on the fair market value or "reasonableness" of the proposed compensation arrangements. You may want to consider using a consultant with the necessary technical expertise and a good understanding of the facts and circumstances pertaining to both sides. A clean and definitive opinion is of little practical value unless the result is an agreement signed by two parties.

Source:

Hobart Collins, "Getting Paid for Taking ER Calls: Who Decides, and How Much Is Fair?" *MGMA Connexion*, V. 6, No. 7, August 2006.

[‡] Internal Revenue Service, IRS Revenue Rule 54-60, 1954-1 CB 241, Jan. 1, 1954.

CHAPTER 3

Governance and Organizational Dynamics

QUESTION 32

I need to develop the bylaws for our medical practice. What should I include?

Bylaws are the rules and guidelines that specify how organizations are structured and governed. Because of their importance and complexity, you may want to work with legal counsel or a consultant in developing them. State laws and the legal business form/entity of your organization (for example, corporation vs. partnership) will also have an impact on your organization's bylaws.

Incorporated practices are required to submit articles of incorporation with a state agency. This document should be fairly broad but have all information required by the particular state. The content typically includes the group's full legal name, the organization's purpose, a statement on how assets will be handled if the organization closes, and the directors' names.

Bylaws should provide more detail than articles of incorporation and be revised as needed. Bylaws provide three important functions:

1. They specify how the organization is structured in terms of membership and duties of its governing board and officers;

2. They outline the rights of governing members, including their right to be notified of meetings, their status on the board, and member indemnification; and

3. They determine the governing procedures on conducting meetings, recording minutes, voting procedures, and the process for revising the bylaws.

Bylaws should include the following information:

➤ Organization's name;

➤ Principal location and other locations;

➤ Statement of purpose;

➤ Members – qualification, termination, meeting schedule and notifications, quorum requirements, action by members, and voting procedures;

➤ Directors – powers, qualifications, election procedures, term, vacancies, resignations, removal, board chairman, quorum of directors, committees, compensation, and minutes of meetings;

➤ Officers – qualifications, duties, selection of officers, terms and term limits, removal of officers, and relationship with the chief executive officer; and

➤ Fiscal matters – finance committee, responsibilities of treasurer, and indemnification.

Sources:

Medical Group Management Association, "Practice Bylaws," *Information Exchange* #5140 (Englewood, CO: Medical Group Management Association, 2002).

Kim Arthur Zeitlin and Susan E. Dorn, *The Nonprofit Board's Guide to Bylaws: Creating a Framework for Effective Governance* (Washington, DC: National Center for Nonprofit Boards, 1996).

QUESTION 33

We are getting large enough that we need to develop a physician board of directors. How can I obtain resources on the responsibilities of the board, the duties of board members, and other board-related matters?

The duties of board members should reflect the role of the governing board and the structure provided in the practice bylaws. The board serves to provide direction and guidance for the organization, letting the administrative positions handle the strategies and day-to-day operations. The roles of the board include:

- ➤ Developing the mission and vision;
- ➤ Identifying organizational goals;
- ➤ Participating in strategic planning;
- ➤ Ensuring executive performance by hiring, setting expectations, and evaluating the organization's chief executive officer or administrator;
- ➤ Overseeing the provision of quality of care;
- ➤ Monitoring the financial health of the organization;
- ➤ Managing external relations with the media, the community, and government; and
- ➤ Conducting self-assessments on board effectiveness.

> ## KEY POINT
>
>  *The board provides direction and guidance for the organization, letting the administrative positions handle the strategies and day-to-day operations.*

Boards typically consist of a chair or president, several officers, and several board members. The president's responsibilities typically include:

- ➤ Presiding over the board and, if applicable, the executive committee;
- ➤ Directing the meetings;

FOR MORE INFORMATION . . .

Two additional sources provide sample board member job descriptions, detailed responsibilities, and other related information:

- ✔ Alys Novak, MBA, *Governing Policies Manual for Medical Practices* (Englewood, CO: Medical Group Management Association, 1996).
- ✔ "Governing Board Compensation," *Information Exchange* #4742 (Englewood, CO: Medical Group Management Association, September 2004).

➤ Ensuring the development of the organizational mission and goals;

➤ Monitoring progress toward meeting the goals; and

➤ Serving as the organization's representative to national associations, local organizations, the media, and other groups.

The vice chair or vice president presides over events during the president's absence. This officer may be president-elect and be "in training" for the role. The secretary records the minutes for the meetings, files annual reports if required by state regulations or other requirements, and maintains the bylaws, articles of organization or constitution, copies of policies, and a record of the board's decisions and agreements. The treasurer reports on the financial health of the organization on a regular basis, ensures that correct and complete financial records are developed and recorded, monitors the financial investments, and chairs the finance committee (if applicable). Some boards combine officer positions, depending on the total number of board members. General board members will support the roles of the board as listed previously, serve on committees, report on issues related to the organization, and participate in the development of the mission and goals.

Members should represent the varying interests and characteristics of the organization and its stakeholders. They should not represent a particular interest group; rather, they should be advocates for the benefit of the complete organization. Members typically serve two- to three-year terms, which overlap to ensure continuity.

The total number of board members will vary depending on the size and complexity of the organization. Groups of less than five physicians might have all of their physicians on the board. Groups with more than five physicians should select a few of them to serve on the board. A 10-physician practice may have three to five board members. If the board grows to seven or more members, you should consider forming an executive committee. Typically consisting of three to four members, the executive committee meets more often than the board, works more closely with the chief executive officer, and provides the board with recommendations on various issues.

Nick Fabrizio, PhD, FACMPE, senior consultant with the MGMA Health Care Consulting Group, suggests that an important consideration related to board responsibilities is the frequency of meetings; members' responsibilities prior to, during, and after board meetings; attendance requirements; and board member evaluations. Physician groups must establish the need to have regularly scheduled meetings, and the outcomes of those meetings should be tracked.

Sources:

Dennis D. Pointer and James E. Orlikoff, *Getting to Great: Principles of Health Care Organization and Governance* (San Francisco: Jossey-Bass, 2002).

"Right-Size Your Group's Board of Directors," *Group Practice Solutions,* March 2003.

Stephen L. Wagner, PhD, FACMPE, "Organization and Operations of Medical Group Practice," in *Physician Practice Management: Essential Operational and Financial Knowledge,* ed. Lawrence F. Wolper, MBA, FACMPE, pp. 39–43 (Sudbury, MA: Jones and Bartlett Publishers, 2005).

QUESTION 34

I would like to implement a program to identify and encourage future physician leaders within our organization. What are other groups doing?

Physicians typically receive little or no education to develop their skills in finance, management, and leadership. Most medical practice physician leaders will continue with clinical responsibilities, potentially limiting their time to learn about and handle organizational leadership responsibilities. Because of these issues, your practice must be willing to devote energy to developing leadership and allow time for physicians to grow into their leadership roles.

Current physician leaders can recognize future leaders as ones who raise issues beyond their immediate personal needs and who recognize issues affecting the organization and the community. According to Richard D. Hansen, MGMA Health Care Consulting Group, good leaders must "know themselves, be respected in their specialty, work well within their group, understand the broader community

---

A CLOSER LOOK...

Physician Leadership Development Case Study

Geisinger Health System in Pennsylvania developed a formal program for sharing the wisdom of the current chief executive officer (CEO). Several sessions were held with a facilitator introducing the program, models of leadership, and the case-based learning process. The CEO joined the group using cases from his experiences or others'. The case is introduced up to the point of the first decision and then opened up to discussion, with the objective of the participants developing their own decision-making skills.

Source: William Gruver and Robert C. Spahr, "Imparting Wisdom to Evolving Leaders," *Physician Executive,* V. 32, No. 3, May/June 2006, pp. 24–29.

of providers, and recognize how their practice serves the community."

Hansen recommends watching for the following six traits in physicians:

- ➤ Maintains high clinical quality;
- ➤ Possesses strong credibility among peers;
- ➤ Shares the organization's mission and values;
- ➤ Asks questions;
- ➤ Offers suggestions; and
- ➤ Volunteers.

Once the potential leaders are identified, help them grow as leaders by appointing them to serve on practice and community committees and encouraging them in their education and learning opportunities.

One way to identify future leaders is to work with interested or selected physicians and encourage them to serve on internal and external committees. Serving on a hospital committee or volunteering in leadership roles with organizations like the Red Cross or United Way gives the physicians an opportunity to develop their skills and determine their own strengths and weaknesses. You will also need to discuss ways in which you collect information on their performance on those committees either through reading minutes, speaking with committee chairs, reviewing committee evaluations, or meeting personally with physicians to discuss their performance and satisfaction with serving on committees.

Your overall goals are to identify potential leaders, assess their performance, build upon their strengths, and develop their areas of needed improvement. This will provide you with an outstanding opportunity to improve the leadership stock you have available in governing your group.

FOR MORE INFORMATION...

Education Resources for Physician Leaders

✔ Medical Group Management Association (www.mgma.com);

✔ American College of Physician Executives (www.acpe.org);

✔ Healthcare Financial Management Association (www.hfma.org);

✔ Universities and medical schools with MD/MBA or health care administration programs; and

✔ Center for Creative Leadership (www.ccl.org).

Consider the following steps to develop effective physician leadership:

➤ Provide a clear definition of the role, including the job description, performance expectations, and the evaluation process.

➤ Discuss the organizational goals and mission to ensure that everyone is working toward the same target as part of the same culture.

➤ Formalize communications to ensure that information is shared fully between leadership and management.

➤ Provide time for the education process and leadership responsibilities. Physicians are not able to develop as effective leaders if their time is committed to clinical services.

➤ Encourage physicians to attend conferences tailored to improving their knowledge base in both general management principles and focused areas such as financial or operational management.

➤ Conduct an orientation session to board activities and responsibilities for new board members.

CHAPTER 3: Governance and Organizational Dynamics   83

> Instill a sense of group responsibility. The most difficult step in the process may be for leaders to place group interests above their personal interests.

Pairing future leaders with mentors will promote sharing of insights and experiences that cannot be gained from formal educational programs. Mentoring can be done informally, such as by having an occasional lunch together, or formally, through regular meetings and discussions.

Sources:

Nick Fabrizio, "Developing Future Physician Leaders in the Health Care Setting," *Group Practice Journal*, V. 50, No. 1, January 2001.

Emile Gauvreau, "On Board: How a Physician Becomes an Effective Member of Your Medical Group's Board of Directors," *MGMA Connexion*, V. 2, No. 2, February 2002.

Richard D. Hansen, "Finding and Developing Physician Leaders," *MGM Update*, V. 39, No. 8, April 2000.

Gregory Mertz, "Effective Physician Governance Is Not an Oxymoron," *MGMA Connexion*, V. 3, No. 1, January 2003.

Dennis D. Pointer and James E. Orlikoff, *Getting to Great: Principles of Health Care Organization and Governance* (San Francisco: Jossey-Bass, 2002).

QUESTION 35

I need ideas for measuring and evaluating the board's performance. What ideas and tools are out there?

You are right to recognize the importance of evaluating your board's performance. Board performance is typically the last aspect of an organization to receive a performance review, but perhaps it is the most vital to an organization. Evaluations are necessary to ensure the continued high performance of the organization, legal and ethical compliance, and commitment to the organization's mission and vision. Self-assessments enable the board to learn and improve itself.

Board evaluations can be done as individual director and officer self-assessments, member reviews of one another, or a complete board evaluation. A board evaluation can be conducted as part of a board meeting using evaluation forms distributed prior to the meeting.

Assessments of individual board members can evaluate:

➤ Commitment to the board;

➤ Appropriate use of their skills and expertise;

➤ Knowledge of the company and its industry;

➤ Percentage of attendance at meetings;

➤ Participation in board meetings and activities; and

➤ General level of preparation.

Assessments of the full board can evaluate its:

➤ Understanding and development of strategy;

➤ Mix of expertise;

➤ Understanding of market trends;

FOR MORE INFORMATION...

The following sources provide sample assessments and additional ideas:

✔ Beaufort B. Longest Jr. and Samuel A. Friede, "The Competent Board: Stitching Together Needed Skills and Knowledge," *Trustee,* V. 55, No. 2, February 2002.

✔ David A. Nadler, "Building Better Boards," *Harvard Business Review,* V. 80, No. 9, May 2004.

✔ Dennis D. Pointer and James E. Orlikoff, *Getting to Great: Principles of Health Care Organization and Governance* (San Francisco: Jossey-Bass, 2002).

✔ Jeffrey A. Sonnenfeld, "What Makes Great Boards Great," *Harvard Business Review,* V. 80, No. 9, September 2002.

> **KEY POINT**
>
> An effective board will develop action plans to improve in those areas identified through performance reviews and define a means of measuring its improvement.

- ➤ Use of external and internal information; and
- ➤ Commitment to the organizational mission and goals.

You can also base the full board assessments on its competence in several areas. Overall board competence depends on the skills and knowledge of its individual members. If competence is found to be lacking in certain areas, the board can provide educational activities to improve it or recruit a new member who has the needed skills.

Boards should show competence in the following areas:

- ➤ **Contextual** – Understanding of the organization's stakeholders, competitors, and status of health care in the community;

- ➤ **Legal and ethical** – General understanding of legal issues, appropriate use of the group's counsel, and adherence to appropriate ethical behavior;

- ➤ **Governance** – Success in following the mission and developing a strategic plan, serving the appropriate role, and advocating for the group in private and public sectors;

- ➤ **Collaborative** – Effectiveness as a team and effectiveness in relationships with external partners; and

➤ **Commercial** – Understanding of general business and financial principles and statements and understanding potential business opportunities.

Boards should also consider their success in relationships with the practice executive and management staff. The governing board should be actively involved in overseeing the administrator and the performance of the group, but it should enable the executive officer to implement the decisions and manage the practice. Board self-assessments should ensure that they are overseeing and not interfering with the executive and the administrative staff.

Remember that the effectiveness of board reviews depends on how they are used as well as how they are conducted. All performance reviews identify areas of needed improvement. An effective board will develop action plans to improve in these areas and define a means of measuring its improvement.

I need to create a mission statement for our group. How do I write one that has meaning?

The mission statement is important for defining your practice, its purpose, and what it wants to accomplish. The statement should guide its goals and major decisions, including the programs and services that it provides or plans. It should challenge the practice team to unite and fulfill the mission together. The mission statement expresses the basic purpose for the organization; from it the vision statement is developed, which provides the goals and the direction that the practice is moving toward. Strategic plans are developed to achieve the vision and fulfill the mission.

In developing a mission statement, it is important to involve as many people as possible. Statements are often created by only a few executives and board members. The more people

A CLOSER LOOK...

Examples of Medical Group Mission Statements

✔ Our mission is to provide high-quality medical care to our patients in an effective and efficient manner consistent with the expectations of our patients and community.

✔ We provide first-rate patient care because we care for every patient.

✔ We are a skilled team dedicated to exceeding public expectations for compassionate, personalized, and scientifically based care for those with brain and behavioral disorders.

Source: Medical Group Management Association, "Strategic Planning and Mission Statements," *Information Exchange* #5362 (Englewood, CO: Medical Group Management Association, May 2004).

---

you involve in the creative process, the more commitment you will have to the mission statement and the more accurately the statement will reflect the true mission and goals of your practice.

The mission statement should be based on answers to the following questions: What is our purpose? Why are we in business? Who do we serve? Allow plenty of time for discussion and debate. Before the mission statement is made final, be sure that your board members, physicians, and staff buy in to it.

When the final mission statement is determined, publicize it. Mission statements are often filed away and forgotten. The mission statement should be printed in practice brochures and made visible on your Website, within your building, and in employee handbooks.

Encourage ongoing discussions: How does each staff member contribute to the mission? How is the mission statement fulfilled? How do the organization's goals support the statement, and what are employees' responsibilities related to accomplishing the goals?

Finally, remember to review the mission statement regularly to ensure that it still adequately reflects your practice and its purpose. A good time to review the group's mission and vision statement is during your strategic planning sessions.

Sources:

Michael Fishbein, "How to Convince Physician Groups to Think and Plan Strategically," ACMPE Professional Paper (Englewood, CO: American College of Medical Practice Executives, August 2005).

"Impromptu: What Rallies Staff Around the Organization's Mission Statement?" *MGMA Connexion*, V. 4, No. 9, October 2004.

Tom Terez, "A Burning Sense of Mission," *Workforce*, V. 82, No. 4, April 2003, web.ebscohost.com/ehost/detail?vid=17&hid=115&sid=16d0c22c-1fff-4ec0-a22e-580be918ff25%40sessionmgr102 (accessed August 17, 2006).

QUESTION 37

I was recently hired as a practice administrator, but I am having difficulty working with the physician leaders. What can I do to improve these relationships so I can do what I was hired to do?

Sometimes difficulties between physicians and administrators arise out of their general differences in education, viewpoints, and styles. Physicians are trained to act independently or on a one-to-one basis with patients. Physicians typically want immediate results and quick feedback and have a scientific perspective. Their priority is the care of their patients. Many administrators prefer to work with a group and believe in building consensus. As such, they are trained to rely on others, use intuition in decision making, and collect data from multiple sources. They are concerned about the long-term impact of decisions. Administrators are also concerned about the financial health of the organization and the morale of employees.

It is important for you to recognize these differences and how they can be used to develop a complementary and collaborative relationship rather than an antagonistic one.

What you may interpret as a physician disagreeing with your decision may be a physician's concern about the impact on patient services. Major decisions should be reached jointly, with you and the physicians presenting your different viewpoints and understanding of the impact of the decision.

The following five-step process can be used to improve the physician–administrator relationship:

1. Identify and agree upon the expectations of your position, the specifics of your role, the goals of the organization, and how these goals will be accomplished. Without clear goals and understanding of the responsibilities, you may concentrate on actions the physicians don't agree with or ignore something they expect you to do.

2. Working with the physicians, develop or revise your job description. Ensure that all expectations are included, along with information on how success will be measured. Expectations and job descriptions should be reviewed and revised on a regular basis.

3. Discuss which areas of responsibility are yours for making decisions unilaterally and which areas require physician involvement.

4. Formalize communication between yourself and the physicians. Schedule regular meetings to discuss the status of the practice, the success in reaching specified goals, and current issues.

5. Stay focused on the agreed-upon responsibilities and goals. Develop protocols with the physicians on how new issues or ideas will be addressed.

As an administrator, you must be able to work with physicians in moving the organization forward. Part of this understanding is realizing that medical leaders are also responsible for preparing the organization for change and monitoring those change initiatives. Physician leaders must be willing and able to develop processes to gather and share data, establish a purpose, communicate with other physicians, and cultivate the core competencies required for group practice success. Facilitating the change process is a time-consuming but vital role for leaders. It is important for the administrator and physicians to understand their roles and sphere of influence within the organization, to respect their boundaries, and to move the organization forward.

Your goal is to develop an effective physician–administrator team; looking at how others make this leadership model a success may help you in your success. Long-term team members Gary Kaplan, MD, FACMPE, and Sarah Patterson, FACMPE, have identified the following keys for successful physician–administrator teams:

➤ Clear goals based on the organization's mission;

➤ Equal status between the physician and the administrator;

➤ Mutual dependence;

➤ Time to know each other and develop trust; and

➤ Shared responsibility and accountability.

In terms of this fourth key, physicians may need more time to develop trust in your capabilities, and you may need more time to understand their style. If you follow the above steps and perform in a manner matching and then exceeding physicians' expectations, you will develop strong relationships with your physician leaders.

Sources:

Nick Fabrizio, "Organizational and Strategic Factors Impact Group Practice Culture," *Performance and Practices of Successful Medical Groups: 2005 Report Based on 2004 Data* (Englewood, CO: Medical Group Management Association, 2005).

Richard D. Hansen, "Group Practice Rx: Physician and Administrator Leadership: Why Different Is Good," *MGMA Connexion*, V. 3, No. 2, February 2003.

Gary S. Kaplan and Sarah Patterson, "The Physician/Administrator Team: An Optimal Model for Leading Medical Practices," *MGMA Connexion*, V. 2, No. 1, January 2002.

Gregory Mertz, "Group Practice Rx: Consider It Job Security," *MGMA Connexion*, V. 3, No. 10, November 2003.

QUESTION 38

Our managing partner wants to be compensated for the time he spends on leadership responsibilities. What's the best way to handle this?

The physician has agreed to take on major responsibilities to serve as a managing partner. Devoting time to his administrative responsibilities will result in a reduction in his clinical time. If your physician compensation model rewards productivity, his compensation will suffer with the shift in responsibilities and time. If your practice wants him to commit time to his administrative duties and not feel penalized financially for it, you may need to make some accommodations.

If you are with a smaller practice, you may not be able to afford additional compensation, especially if the revenue declines due to reductions in the managing partners' clinical productivity. Two other options are changing the compensation system so that the physician is not penalized and rotating the responsibilities among all the physicians.

If you represent a larger practice, the additional compensation may not be as much of a factor. The actual compensation amount will depend on factors such as the amount of time the physician commits to the responsibility, the size of the practice and the complexity of the partner's responsibilities, and the potential loss of income due to decreased clinical productivity.

MGMA conducted an *Information Exchange* (an informal survey) asking groups if their managing partners and medical directors received additional compensation and, if so, how they determined the amount. In practices where physicians spent 5 percent or less of their time on administrative responsibilities, 55 percent received no additional compensation, while 32 percent received a predetermined amount each month. When the time commitment increased to between 5 percent and 10 percent, about 50 percent of the practices provided a specific amount. In practices providing compensation, physicians committing 10 percent of their time averaged $2,155 a month beyond the compensation received for clinical services.

Physician leaders spending 50 percent to 100 percent of their time on administrative responsibilities were most frequently compensated by straight salary. Generally only the largest practices (averaging 85 physicians) had a physician devoting a majority of his or her time to these responsibilities. In the MGMA *Management Compensation Survey: 2005 Report Based on 2004 Data,* the median compensation for the title of physician chief executive officer/president was $292,846, and the median compensation for medical directors was $228,764.

Sources:

Richard D. Hansen, "Finding and Developing Physician Leaders," *MGM Update,* V. 39, No. 8, April 2000.

Mary Mourar, "Compensating Physicians for Administrative Responsibilities," *MGMA e-Connexion,* Issue 18, October 2002.

Medical Group Management Association, *Management Compensation Survey: 2005 Report Based on 2004 Data* (Englewood, CO: Medical Group Management Association, 2005).

Suz Redfearn, "Do Managerial Roles Pay: Extra Duties Can Complicate Compensation," *Physicians Practice,* V. 12, No. 4, May/June 2002.

Some of our physicians and employees are concerned about implementing an EHR and the changes it will mean. How can I help them through these changes?

Your group is probably similar to most organizations in that some individuals look forward to change while others prefer things the way they are now. It is natural for people to be concerned about change, with the unknowns that it can bring. However, some people react with more anxiety and more resistance.

Understanding the reasons for opposing change may help you to help your employees. These individuals may have fears related to:

- Concerns about losing their jobs;
- A previous bad experience with technology or other change;
- Being humiliated if they are too slow to handle the change; or
- Not feeling in control with the change and related decision making.

The following six-step process can help others adapt to change:

1. Prepare for change by explaining the limitations of the current system and what new options are available. Start physicians and employees thinking about potential changes for the better. Individuals may be more welcoming to ideas that they are aware of, rather than having new ideas sprung on them.

2. Clearly identify the reason for the change, the benefits it will bring, and how it will be implemented to make the transition as smooth as possible.

3. Determine what motivates the change resistors and relate the change to their interests. For example: "If we implement the EHR, you won't have to spend time looking for lost records." Common motivators in health care include making more money, eliminating boring or repetitive tasks, increasing patient satisfac-

tion or safety, and increasing efficiency to decrease overtime.

4. Discuss how the change relates to the big picture. For example, the EHR supports the agreed-upon vision and goals of the group to implement technology to improve patient safety.

5. Build your case using quantifiable measures and how they will be improved. An example of a quantifiable measure is X number of hours each day to pull paper records.

6. Be prepared to respond to any objection before it is raised.

You can use staff or department meetings to implement these steps. The involvement and team building during the meetings will increase acceptance of the change. Allow plenty of time for discussion, listening to and addressing concerns, discussing how the change will improve operations, and soliciting ideas on ways to ease the implementation process. Explain how you will ensure that adequate training will be provided to everyone.

Continue to meet with those resisting change to offer reassurances. As the change is implemented, offer them additional training, information, and support. Express your confidence that they will eventually wonder why they were concerned about the new system.

Nick Fabrizio, PhD, FACMPE, also suggests that another effective strategy is to identify your physician champion who will be the physician representative to lead the implementation. This person may also be the physician "techie" who will be excited, willing, and able to drive the implementation plans forward.

Your implementation efforts will improve once you identify this physician techie, who will be charged with leading the implementation for the physicians, ensuring that the technology meets its stated clinical purpose, and identifying and working with physician outliers who need additional training and support in using the new technology.

Another good strategy is to employ a buddy system whereby the more technologically advanced physicians work with those who are less advanced on a one-to-one basis. The "expert" user will help their physician "buddy" by answering their questions, mentoring them during selected clinical hours, or having them shadow their clinical sessions to observe their processes. All of these factors are designed to improve the implementation efforts and shorten the learning curve.

Sources:

Vicky Bradford, "Know-How: Making Your Case for Change," *MGMA Connexion,* V. 3, No. 7, August 2003.

Gary C. Hamill, "Quick Tip: Team-Building Helps Employees Embrace – Not Fear – Change," *MGMA e-Connexion,* Issue 65, November 2004.

CHAPTER 4

Human Resources Management

QUESTION 40

One of the partners in our group is retiring soon. Is there a checklist of some type to aid in the process to ensure a smooth transition for both the retiring partner and the practice?

The biggest retirement issue you'll have to deal with is the partner buyout. According to Bruce Johnson, JD, MPA, principal, MGMA Health Care Consulting Group, the cost of buying out a retiring physician used to include the stock purchase of the retiring physician's shares based on the depreciated book value of the practice's hard assets paid over a five-year period with interest. Buyouts also included payments of "deferred compensation" equal to a portion, say 80 percent, of the retiring physician's average W-2 compensation over the previous three years, with value considered an exchange for a share of the physician's accounts receivable plus a premium for goodwill.

Today many groups have a difficult time living up to such terms while staying financially healthy, according to Johnson. Even though the buyout may have seemed reasonable when drafted years earlier, many of those formulas can cause substantial financial hardship to the practice and the physicians who remain. The cash flow and other implications of these buyout arrangements may force the practice to either revisit the buyout or risk destruction of the group itself.

A medical practice can avoid the trap of unrealistic physician buyout terms by carefully reviewing its basic legal documents, including the shareholders' "buy/sell" agreements, employment and partnership agreements, facility corporation documents, and other partnership agreements. Physician compensation formulas also may need review.

A CLOSER LOOK...

Checklist for physician's retirement

Task	Timeline	✔ (when completed)
Settle all buyout issues.		
Agree on the actual retirement date.		
Notify staff of the retirement and the transition plan.		
Send notice to the physician's patients and provide them with names of other physicians. Check state laws for notification requirements.		
Determine how the physician's patient charts will be managed (typically retained in the practice).		
Notify Medicare, Medicaid, and third-party payers.		
Notify referring physicians.		
Contact your malpractice insurer and set up tail coverage.		
Determine ownership of accounts receivable after the physician's departure. Is it specified in the contract?		
Remove the physician's name from the answering service, phone system, marketing materials, and so on.		

Johnson also offers the following tips when preparing for a physician's retirement:

➤ Discuss the physician's retirement and the practice's slowdown options in strategic planning sessions;

➤ Make it clear that the interests of the entire group are paramount to those of individuals;

➤ Create practice buyout options based on realistic value;

- Make sure buyout terms focus on real money (that is, the physician's personal accounts receivable);

- Provide that the group can lengthen the buyout terms if two or more physicians are retiring at once;

- Establish clear rules regarding physicians who want to slow down before retiring, which might include fewer perks, reduced compensation for less participation in call coverage, and termination as a shareholder/partner;

- Don't expect substantial reductions in operational costs; and

- Revisit the buyout terms and the group's financial health related to those terms at least every two years.

Physician employment agreements should include statements regarding how much notification a physician must provide the practice before departing. These agreements should be reviewed for this and other issues such as deferred compensation, retirement benefits, and malpractice tail coverage.

Once this process is completed, take note of the lessons learned during the transition and apply them as you prepare for the next physician's retirement. The Physician Retirement and Practice Transition Self-Assessment Tool from the MGMA Website (www.mgma.com) can help you prepare. Review all physicians' contracts to remind yourself of their terms and issues that you may need to prepare for now.

Sources:

Bob Redling, "It Is Never Too Soon to Plan for Physician Retirement," *MGM Update*, V. 39, No. 12, June 2000.

James D. Wall, "A Must-Do List for the Departing Physician," *Family Practice Management*, V. 12, No. 9, October 2005, www.aafp.org/fpm/20051000/54amus.html (accessed August 29, 2006).

Gail Garfinkel Weiss, "How to Close a Practice," *Medical Economics,* January 9, 2004, www.memag.com/memag (accessed August 10, 2006).

QUESTION 41

I need to write a policy regarding sexual harassment. Are there any sample policies that I can use?

The following sexual harassment policy is from MGMA's *HR Policies & Procedures Manual for Medical Practices*, by Courtney Price, PhD (Englewood, CO: Medical Group Management Association, 2007). The author advises that practices make appropriate adaptations to the sample according to the group's management philosophy, organizational needs, staff size, and state requirements.

Complying with Employment Laws
Policy 2.04
Workplace Harassment Policy

The Practice is committed to providing a working environment in which its employees are treated with courtesy, respect, and dignity. The Practice does not tolerate nor condone any actions by any individuals that constitute any kind of harassment, particularly sexual harassment of an employee.

PROCEDURES

1. The Human Resources manager shall educate, in various ways, including through seminars and the employee handbook, all managers, supervisors, and employees on the medical practice's workplace harassment policy.

2. This education shall define sexual harassment as unwelcome sexual advances, requests for sexual favors, and other verbal, nonverbal, written, or physical conduct of a sexual nature by employees, supervisors, clients, or contractors where such conduct is either made an explicit or implicit term or condition of employment, is used as the basis for employment decisions, or has the purpose or effect of substantially interfering with the employee's work by creating an intimidating, hostile, or offensive working environment.

3. Deliberate, repeated, and unsolicited comments with sexual overtones, sexual jokes or ridicule, physical gestures or actions of a sexual nature, and solicitations for sexual favors, offensive comments about one's race, age, disability, or sexual orientation are violations of this policy and subject the offender to discipline, which may include discharge.

4. A complaint of a hostile work environment/harassment situation should be directed to the HR manager, who shall promptly and fully investigate the complaint to ensure compliance with this policy. Confidentiality shall be maintained to the maximum extent possible, consistent with the need to investigate the complaint.

Supervisor Worksheet for Dealing with Workplace Harassment Situation

Name of employee/complainant:

_____
_____
_____

Date of complaint:

_____
_____
_____

Name of supervisor/investigator and date of interview:

_____
_____
_____

Allegation of workplace harassment, as described by the complainant:

_____
_____
_____

Corrective action requested by the complainant (even if the complainant does not want any corrective action taken, you must ensure that the workplace harassment stops):

_____

_____

Alleged harasser's(s') description of the situation:

_____

_____

Additional information (documentation, witnesses, previous situations):

_____

_____

The names of staff members to contact for additional information or assistance:

_____

_____

Name of Human Resources manager/designee from whom you sought counsel:

_____

_____

Your analysis of the situation:

_____

_____

CHAPTER 4: Human Resources Management

Your action plan, including corrective action:

_____
_____
_____
_____

Follow-up action and date for follow-up:

_____
_____
_____
_____

QUESTION 42

Has anyone calculated the average cost of turnover when you lose key employees? Does MGMA track turnover ratios in medical practices?

The total cost for replacing an employee is estimated to be 50 percent to 150 percent of the annual salary of the position, with the higher percentages for managerial staff. That means it can cost an organization up to $75,000 to replace a $50,000-a-year worker. These percentages include all related costs such as recruiting, hiring and training, using temporary employees during transitions, and lost productivity during the first six months of employment. Overall, it is more costly to replace staff than to retain your current staff. Therefore, a practice should continually monitor its turnover rates by job classification and then set realistic goals and monitor performance yearly.

MGMA tracks employee turnover rates in the annual *Performance and Practices of Successful Medical Groups* report:

Position	% of turnover
Receptionists and medical records staff	20.00%
Nursing and clinical support staff	12.50%
Billing/collections and data entry staff	7.69%
Administrative staff	0.00%
Physicians and nonphysician providers	2.96%

Source: *Performance and Practices of Successful Medical Groups: 2005 Report Based on 2004 Data* (Englewood, CO: Medical Group Management Association, 2005).

If your turnover ratios are higher than these averages, you should determine the reasons for the turnover, the degree of employee satisfaction in general, and the steps you can take to reduce turnover.

Are you asking departing employees their reasons for leaving the practice? Establishing a standardized exit interview survey will help reveal issues that lead to employees leaving the practice and uncover any trends in turnover. In turn, this will help you to develop a plan to reduce future turnover. Asking a few questions may provide insight on issues within the practice that may be affecting employee satisfaction. The interviewer should be someone other than the immediate supervisor. Questions can include:

- ➤ What influenced your decision to leave?
- ➤ How could the group have made your job more manageable or rewarding?
- ➤ Was the employee orientation and on-the-job training adequate or could these have been improved?
- ➤ How has management responded to your concerns?
- ➤ Were the salary and benefits adequate for the responsibilities assigned?
- ➤ What did you like and dislike about this practice, its work processes, and your interpersonal relationships?

Employee satisfaction surveys distributed to all employees will also show areas of concern that can be addressed. Sample satisfaction surveys can be obtained from the MGMA Information Center (1-877-275-6462, ext. 887), within numerous periodicals and books, or from your fellow peers in human resources management.

If you are determined to improve employee retention, you should also look at what you offer. Employees are more apt to remain in a practice that:

- Offers attractive salaries and benefits;
- Accepts flexible scheduling;
- Supports continuing education and advancement;
- Encourages open communication, including regular meetings;
- Has effective relationships among supervisors and physicians;
- Listens to employees' suggestions and ideas; and
- Offers a sense of community within the workplace.

Recruiting the right person for the position and practice culture will also increase retention. It is important to have a thorough recruitment process to analyze the position and skills required and to provide adequate time to review candidates' qualifications and personalities.

Understanding and managing an organization's culture (its attitudes, beliefs, and communications) will also decrease the reasons that employees leave organizations. Through a better understanding of the issues related to certain job classifications, managers can play a more active role in understanding the issues related to those duties and tasks. This in turn will help employees and managers to communicate more effectively and eventually decrease turnover rates.

Sources:

Gary Alexander, "Know-How: Finder and Keepers: Locating and Retaining the Right Staff," *MGMA Connexion*, V. 5, No. 3, March 2005.

Brad Dunevitz, "Treat Employees as Assets, Not Costs: Highly Portable Employees Worth Keeping," *MGM Update*, V. 39, No. 5, March 2000.

Bob Redling, "Departing Employees' Comments Can Help Cut Turnover," *MGM Update*, V. 38, No. 18, September 1999.

Nick Fabrizio, "Why Employees Resist Change in Medical Group Practice Acquisitions," *MGMA Journal*, March/April 1999.

QUESTION 43

I want to develop an incentive/bonus system for our practice administrator. Do you have any advice on how to structure it?

A majority of practices (73.2 percent) responding to the MGMA *Information Exchange* (an informal survey) "Administrator Incentive Plans" have an administrator/executive compensation system with a bonus or incentive component. The type of bonus or incentive plan varies as follows:

Type of incentive	Percent
Bonus based on practice profit	51.2%
Raise based on merit	47.9%
Discretionary cash award for exemplary performance	45.5%
Profit sharing	36.4%
Discretionary noncash award for exemplary performance	4.1%

Elements of the administrator's incentive system should include the following:

➤ Goals aligned with the practice's overall goals and strategy;

➤ Both cost-reducing goals and income-producing goals to balance changes within the practice;

➤ Reasonable job expectations that are consistent with the job description; and

➤ Realistic incentives and goals that can be clearly defined and measured.

Examples of incentive plans from the MGMA *Information Exchange* respondents include the following:

1. The administrator is eligible for a bonus of up to 60 percent of the base salary, with 75 percent of the bonus based on achievement of the financial goals established for that year and 25 percent based on operational goals.

2. Specific goals for the practice administrator are:

➤ Maintaining overtime below X percent of total hours;

➤ Maintaining accounts receivable days at XX;

➤ Developing strategies to better manage indigent care;

➤ Developing a plan to reduce paper and improve efficiency of records management; and

➤ Developing and beginning the implementation of a marketing plan with a measurement system for results.

3. The CEO will receive a bonus determined by a vote of the board of directors, which will be based on performance of the duties and the following goals:

➤ Managing financial performance to meet financial goals as determined by the CEO and the board;

➤ Managing human resources to minimize turnover and promote job satisfaction (as identified by employee satisfaction surveys);

A CLOSER LOOK...

Ideas for administrator performance measures for performance reviews and incentive plans

- ✔ Patient satisfaction or complaints;
- ✔ Employee satisfaction or turnover rates;
- ✔ Physician satisfaction;
- ✔ Collection percentages;
- ✔ Days in accounts receivable;
- ✔ Appointment wait times;
- ✔ Operating costs; and
- ✔ New revenue sources.

Source: "Practice Manager Performance Measures," *MGMA Connexion*, V. 6, No. 1, January 2006.

> Developing and implementing a strategic plan to recruit a new physician to provide new cardiology services;

> Managing external relationships to increase referrals; and

> Maintaining turnover rates at X percent by job classification per year.

4. The administrator will receive a percentage of a potential bonus of $XX,XXX, based on the score achieved in this year's performance review.

The structure of the incentive plan must match the practice's culture and structure; be mutually agreeable to the physicians, board of directors, and administrator; and provide the incentives to attain practice goals. The plan should also be reviewed yearly to ensure it is achieving its intended purpose.

CHAPTER 4: Human Resources Management **111**

Sources:

"Buck the Trend, Investigate Defined Incentives for Your Top Manager," *Financial Management Strategies for Medical Offices*, April 2002.

Medical Group Management Association, "Administrator Incentive Plans," *Information Exchange* #6530 (Englewood, CO: Medical Group Management Association, January 2006).

QUESTION 44

I am interested in learning what methods organizations are using to effectively recruit new physicians. Also, should we offer production-based compensation or a guaranteed salary?

There are several steps you can take to successfully recruit a physician that matches your practice's culture and goals:

1. **Develop a recruitment plan, budget, and team.**

    Identify the individuals for the team, selecting a mix of positions and responsibilities to include different viewpoints. The recruitment team should include a recruitment coordinator and someone with the authority to negotiate and close a contract. Decide if a recruitment firm will be used.

2. **Determine the profile of the ideal new physician.**

    Will s/he be just out of residency or will s/he have more experience? Besides specialty, determine what other skills, licenses, and certifications the ideal candidate will have. The team should agree on the basic package, salary, and benefits that will be offered to candidates. Team members will also be involved in orienting and mentoring the new physician.

3. **Get to know the candidate.**

    Conducting a preliminary screening of each candidate saves time and money. Review the candidate's curriculum vitae and send out your practice's promo-

A CLOSER LOOK...

Compensation for Recently Hired Physicians

In years past, practices typically offered a guaranteed salary for the first year or two. This prevented the new physician from worrying about producing enough while still learning about the practice and developing a patient base. In recent years, practices have been steering away from a 100 percent salary guarantee and toward plans that provide incentives. Today, many practices use a combination of a base salary and production incentive. As the new physician's collections increase, the salary increases. If collections don't reach the targets, the base pay drops. This plan still requires base salary guarantees during an extended orientation period and setting realistic targets for collections.

Source: "For a New Physician, Hold the Salary and Give an Incentive," *Group Practice Solutions,* November 2003.

---

tional materials. Use a telephone interview to screen candidates for:

- Geographic compatibility;
- Medical interests and strengths;
- Personal and recreational issues;
- Adequacy of your compensation package; and
- Agreement in practice and candidate's goals.

4. Verify the candidate's credentials and background.

Have the applicant sign a release of information prior to this check. Confirm his or her education, certification, licensure, work history and hospital affiliations, legal history, credit history, and references.

Parts of the reference check may be best conducted by the medical director or managing partner. During the reference check, ask about the candidate's reliability, clinical competence, relationships with others, personality, malpractice issues, problems affecting his or her work, and whether the reference recommends the candidate.

5. **Meet with the candidate.**

    Bring the candidate and his or her family to the practice for a site visit. This is your opportunity to determine if there's a match in personality, culture, goals, and skills and needs between the candidate and your practice. This visit must be comprehensive.

    The candidate's spouse or partner will play a key role in retention, so it is important to include that person in the interview process. Handle all logistics of airfare, lodging, and ground transportation. Plan for activities the spouse or partner can pursue while the candidate meets with staff. The agenda for the site visit should be full yet allow plenty of opportunity for interaction. During the interview, ask as many open-ended questions as possible.

    You should also be selling the practice to the candidate – what makes your practice so great to work for and why the community is a great place to live in. Highlight the compensation and benefits package as well as buy-in and partnership opportunities.

6. **Develop a budget.**

    Nick Fabrizio, PhD, FACMPE, senior consultant, MGMA Health Care Consulting Group, recommends that groups develop a yearly recruitment budget. Budget categories should include hotel accommodations for two nights per visit per candidate, food, ground transportation, entertainment expenses, and the cost of bringing the candidates spouse or significant other.

A CLOSER LOOK...

Steps to take before recruiting

✔ Document the reasons for hiring;
✔ Determine the profile of the ideal candidate;
✔ Provide adequate resources for recruitment;
✔ Promote the open position in print ads, on Internet sites, at medical schools, and in other ways;
✔ Prepare a list of interview questions;
✔ Anticipate candidates' questions;
✔ Develop promotional materials for the practice;
✔ Have a contract in place; and
✔ In addition to traditional recruitment techniques, such as print ads, direct mail, and networking, investigate new ways to recruit candidates, such as through Internet ads and e-mail.

---

7. **Close the deal.**

    If the practice and candidate are in agreement, offer the contract in person, if possible, or via overnight mail. Follow up with a phone call to discuss any questions the candidate may have. To close on the offer:

    ➢ Keep the dialogue continuous, open, and honest during the negotiation;

    ➢ Provide a reasonable time beyond which your offer is void (30 days is typical);

    ➢ Offer a second visit if the contract is unsigned after 30 days; and

    ➢ Consider providing a signing bonus or reimbursing relocation expenses if your practice is in a hard-to-recruit location or the candidate's specialties are in high demand.

Successful physician recruitment and retention require an investment of time and resources. But the results will be a long and successful relationship between physician and practice.

Sources:

Billy D. Adkisson and Seven Bjelich, "Maximizing Physician Recruitment Programs," *Healthcare Executive*, V. 19, No. 5, September/October 2004.

"For a New Physician, Hold the Salary and Give an Incentive," *Group Practice Solutions*, November 2003.

Lisa H. Schneck, "The Art of Physician Recruitment and Retention," *MGM Update*, V. 39, No. 11, June 2000.

Carol Westfall, "Retaining Physicians," *Click*, October 2003.

QUESTION 45

One of our physicians will be leaving the practice, and I will need to hire a locum tenens physician. Do you have information on contracting with one, including how to bill for services, hospital privileges, and so on?

Medicare does accept claims for services provided by locum tenens physicians; however, Medicare views a locum tenens physician as a substitute for the regular physician. Therefore, the claim should be submitted under the regular physician's Medicare number, and payment will be made to that physician. Your practice will then pay the locum, either on a fixed per diem amount or an hourly contract rate.

The Centers for Medicare & Medicaid Services (CMS) *Medicare Carrier Manual* includes the specific requirements under the section "Payment Under Locum Tenens Arrangements." The regulations limit the locum's services to 60 days and specifies that modifier Q6, services furnished by a locum tenens physician, is attached to the appropriate claims.

Prior to the locum tenens starting in your practice, you should take care of several details:

> Notify the physician's patients of his or her impending departure and that a qualified substitute physician will be available.

> Investigate the locum's credentials to ensure s/he is licensed in the state and certified or otherwise qualified to serve in the specialty needed.

> Check the Office of Inspector General (OIG) List of Excluded Individuals/Entities (www.oig.hhs.gov/fraud/exclusions/listofexcluded.html) to make certain the locum has not been suspended or excluded from any government health program.

> Confirm that the locum has malpractice coverage, including tail coverage that will protect the practice after his or her departure. Physicians hired through most placement agencies have coverage provided by the agency.

> Obtain hospital privileges with area hospitals; this process may be lengthy and must be started early.

Sources:

Charlene McGinty and Sandra Herron, "Take Heed When Taking Off: Be Careful When Hiring a Substitute Physician," *Physicians Practice*, V. 14, No. 8, September 2004, www.physicianspractice.com.

Dorrie Westman, "Accept a Substitute: But Make Sure to File Claims for Locum Tenens Services Appropriately," *MGMA Connexion*, V. 4, No. 1, January 2004.

QUESTION 46

Do you have resources that would help me create a physician retention plan? What are typical physician turnover rates?

You're a step ahead of your peers in developing a retention plan. Although many practices have physician recruitment plans, very few have retention plans. However, with the proper retention plan, the recruitment process won't be needed very often.

During the MGMA audio conference "Physician Recruitment Update," Nelson Tilden, PhD, MBA, provided the following advice for developing a physician retention plan:

- ➤ **Establish a board policy.** The elements of this policy should be put in writing and approved by the board. Establish goals and objectives.

- ➤ **Designate responsibility.** Specific individuals should monitor, manage, and be held responsible for retention duties. Consider establishing a retention committee in a larger practice.

- ➤ **Recruit wisely.** Many of the issues that lead physicians to leave a practice can be discovered through careful screening, assessment, and interviewing of potential recruits.

- ➤ **Provide a thorough physician orientation program.** Show newcomers the community, including the hospitals, clinic sites, and nursing homes that the practice deals with.

- ➤ **Introduce newcomers to other physicians in the community.** Include the physicians they will deal with for referrals or consultations, as well as other key players from outside the practice, such as the administrators of referring facilities.

- ➤ **Develop a marketing plan.** Show the newcomer how the medical practice will make his or her practice known to the community.

- ➤ **Implement a mentor/buddy system for the physician.** The heart and soul of a retention plan is the exposure of the newly recruited physician to a network of potential advisers and confidants. Duties can be shared, and mentors can be matched by age, gender, specialty, or interest area. Do not choose someone superior or subordinate to the physician as a mentor.

➤ **Implement a mentor/buddy system for the physician's spouse.** Finding someone of the spouse's gender to help adapt to the community is especially important when the physician is relocating to the area.

➤ **Help the physician and family integrate into the community.** Some communities, especially small ones, are harder to break into, so take extra steps, such as making more introductions during orientation, if needed.

➤ **Provide encouragement.** Offer frequent comments to the new physician on a job well done.

➤ **Interview all physicians who leave.** Even weeks or months after they leave, former practice members can frankly reveal issues that other newcomers might experience.

➤ **Continue to evaluate your turnover rate.** List the reasons that physicians give for leaving the practice. Over time you may discover what is leading to voluntary physician departures.

A proper orientation program is vital to successful physician retention. If your orientation period consists of one day to sign papers, meet everyone, provide an overwhelming amount of information, and give a quick tour of the facility, your new physician will start off without the knowledge needed to successfully integrate into your practice. A comprehensive orientation program lasts three to five days and covers an extensive list of topics. (See the New Physician Orientation Checklist.)

New Physician Orientation Checklist

Use this form to designate *who* in your practice will be responsible for orienting new physicians in each listed area. This checklist can help create an orientation process or assess the current orientation process. Using abbreviations in the legend below, note *who* takes care of each item and *when* each item is to be done.

Source material for this tool originally appeared in the March 2003 *MGMA Connexion*. For more information on this topic, search for physician orientation in the MGMA on-line Article Archive.

Legend

Who

A	Administrator
HR	Human resources function
M	Mentor
P	Physician
S	Supervisor or medical director

When

B	Before the first day
D	First day
W	First week
FM	First month
F	Follow-up after first month

Organization	Who	When	What
			History
			Mission
			Vision
			Organizational philosophy
			Organizational objectives
			Organizational structure
			Industry
			Products and services
			Customers
			Physician's department
			Facilities

Compensation	Who	When	What
			Pay schedule
			Time card
			Salary reviews
			Payroll deductions
			Forms
			Charities
			Workers' compensation

Benefits	Who	When	What
			Medical plan
			Dental plan
			Life insurance
			Pension plan
			Credit union
			Savings plan
			Incentive programs
			Service and recognition awards
			Employee purchases
			Training and development programs
			Profit sharing

Leave and holidays	Who	When	What
			Holidays
			Leave policy
			Vacation
			Jury duty

Health and safety	Who	When	What
			Emergency procedures
			First aid
			Accident protocols
			Child care program
			Wellness program
			Employee assistance program

Security	Who	When	What
			Security procedures
			Restricted areas
			Confidentiality
			Name badge
			After-hours procedure
			Keys
			Drug testing
			Intranet password
			Electronic medical record password

Internal communications	Who	When	What
			Organizational newsletter
			Organization bulletin board
			Employee handbook
			Voice mail
			E-mail

Transportation	Who	When	What
			Carpooling and ride sharing
			Parking
			Travel policies and expenses
			Parking permits or restricted areas

Performance	Who	When	What
			Physician expectations
			Quality
			Ethical standards
			Conflict of interest
			Dress code
			Telephone procedures and courtesy
			Promotions
			Disciplinary process
			Causes for termination
			Equal opportunity
			Sexual harassment
			Accepting gifts

A CLOSER LOOK...

The average annual turnover rate for doctors in U.S. medical groups was 6.4 percent in 2005, according to a survey conducted by the American Medical Group Association and Cejka Search.

Source: Michael Romano, "Doc *Turnover* Rate Falls: Study," *Modern Healthcare*, V. 36, No. 11, March 13, 2006.

According to the same survey, the common reasons for physician turnover were:

- ✔ Practice issues (44 percent);
- ✔ Compensation and location (21 percent); and
- ✔ Reasons involving spouse (14 percent).

Source: Joan Rose, "On Finance and Practice: Group Practices Look for Ways to Retain Physicians," *Medical Economics*, May 5, 2006, www.memag.com/memag (accessed August 10, 2006).

It is also important to provide adequate training for the newly recruited physician. According to MGMA Consultant Nick Fabrizio, PhD, FACMPE, in addition to following an orientation checklist, practices should also assign a "physician buddy" to that person to help answer questions that arise from the checklist and to help with the assimilation process. The buddy can also help the new physician with understanding the practice's policies and procedures and the clinical protocols the group follows. In practices that use an EMR, it is crucial to tailor the training to that physician's learning style. While some of this training can be provided by the group's expert user, the physician buddy can provide hands-on assistance during a patient visit.

An additional tool in managing physician retention is an occasional physician satisfaction survey. This tool will help you assess physicians' current satisfaction with the practice and potential areas of concern. MGMA *Information Exchange* #4750, "Physician Satisfaction Survey," offers several sample surveys.

Sources:

Susan Wendling Alo, "Developing and Implementing a Successful Physician Orientation Program," ACMPE Professional Paper (Englewood, CO: American College of Medical Practice Executives, May 2002).

Nelson Tilden, PhD, MHA, MGMA audio conference "Physician Recruitment Update" as quoted in Bob Redling, "More Than Salary Necessary to Keep Physicians on Board," *MGM Update,* V. 40, No. 6, March 2001.

QUESTION

I just calculated that I have five full-time-equivalent (FTE) employees per physician in my primary care practice. How does this number compare with other practices? How do I know if I have the right number of staff for the practice?

Number of staff per physician in group practices is tracked in the annual MGMA *Cost Survey Report* and the *Performance and Practices of Successful Medical Groups:*

Total support FTE staff per FTE physician

Practice	Better performing groups	Others
Primary care single specialty	4.60	3.81
Medicine single specialty	5.46	4.20
Surgical single specialty	6.36	4.43

Note: FTE = full-time-equivalent

Source: Medical Group Management Association, *Performance and Practices of Successful Medical Groups: 2005 Report Based on 2004 Data* (Englewood, CO: Medical Group Management Association, 2005).

Because your numbers are a little high compared to other practices, your first instinct may be to make some staff reductions. However, you should apply the concept of rightsizing to determine staffing levels for your practice. Rightsizing is the systematic process of reviewing employee numbers, tasks, and work processes to determine the appropriate number and mix of staff needed to meet medical practice goals. Rightsizing involves quantitative and qualitative analyses to answer two key questions: "Do you have the right staff?" and "Are they doing the right things?"

> ## KEY POINT
>
>  *Rightsizing is the systematic process of reviewing employee numbers, tasks, and work processes to determine the appropriate number and mix of staff needed to meet medical practice goals. Rightsizing involves quantitative and qualitative analyses to answer two key questions: "Do you have the right staff?" and "Are they doing the right things?"*

According to David N. Gans, MSHA, CMPE, coauthor of *Rightsizing: Appropriate Staffing for Your Medical Practice*, many factors affect staffing; these include the types of professional and ancillary services, the relative complexity of patient services provided, and physician preference. Knowing that various staffing models exist helps the practice administrator understand that there are many potential answers to the question, "How many employees are enough?"

Analysis of MGMA data on staffing numbers and financial ratios shows that medical practices have decreased financial performance at the lowest and often at the highest levels of staffing. If a practice has too few employees, it isn't maximizing provider productivity, and revenue is reduced. If there are too many employees, their salary and benefit expenses outweigh the benefits of increased productivity.

Deborah Walker Keegan, PhD, FACMPE, coauthor of *Rightsizing: Appropriate Staffing for Your Medical Practice*, recommends a three-step process to evaluating your staffing levels:

1. Benchmark your clinical and administrative staffing levels, staffing costs per physician, and salary and benefit costs as a percentage of net medical revenue.

If you use data from *Performance and Practices of Successful Medical Groups,* you will compare your practice with better performing groups, rather than the general group practice population reported in the MGMA *Cost Survey Report.* Better performers tend to have higher staff costs per physician but lower expenses as a percent of net medical revenue.

2. Analyze your staffing deployment model. Do you have a care team for each physician, or do the clinical and administrative staff serve several different physicians? Do you feel that the staffing model best serves the physicians? Your physicians' preferences will affect their productivity and, therefore, the total practice revenue.

3. Assess your business operations. Are they streamlined and efficient? Are there delays due to overloaded positions? Are there means of combining steps? Is there an emphasis on patient service that will also decrease the number of patient phone calls and delays in payment?

In the article "More than Staffing Ratios: What To Consider when Evaluating the Need for Information Technology Employees," Nick Fabrizio, PhD, FACMPE, stresses that as part of the administrator's due diligence, in addition to benchmarking your staff based on MGMA staffing ratios, it is important to document, analyze, and understand workflow processes. Because of the rapid developments and use of technology in medical groups, it is increasingly important to understand how technology affects all job categories. Technology changes the way people work, and managers should understand how their internal processes will be affected and how staffing ratios might change depending on how your practice adopts those technologies.

Completing the rightsizing analysis will help ensure that your practice is operating in an efficient manner. Just looking at your staff numbers compared with other practices doesn't provide the understanding that you need to maximize practice performance. As Dave Gans says, rightsizing is "the right number of staff, in the right place, with the right skills, at the right cost, with the right behavior, the right rewards, and the right outcomes – no more, no less."

Sources:

David N. Gans, "On the Edge: Rightsize – Do Not Downsize," *MGMA Connexion*, V. 3, No. 1, January 2003.

Deborah Walker Keegan, "Quick Tip: Don't Play the Numbers Game with Your Care Team – Get the Right Staff for the Right Work," *MGMA e-Connexion*, Issue 81, July 2005.

Nick A. Fabrizio, PhD, FACMPE, "More than Staffing Ratios: What to Consider When Evaluating the Need for Information Technology Employees," *MGMA Connexion*, V. 6, No. 4, May/June 2006.

QUESTION 48

One of our physicians has announced that he would like to retire in a few years and go part-time in the meantime. How can I handle his request for a part-time schedule in a manner that is agreeable to the other physicians?

Physicians have several reasons for requesting a part-time or reduced schedule, from approaching retirement to demands related to family commitments. Accepting this option will help the practice retain a talented physician, but it can also cause resentment in other physicians and have negative budgetary implications.

Several issues must be dealt with prior to allowing a physician to begin a part-time schedule:

➤ Define *part-time:* What is the minimum number of hours that a physician will be allowed to work? What is the maximum number of hours compared to the practice's normal work week that will be defined as part-time?

A CLOSER LOOK...

Compensation methodology for part-time physicians

Productivity	47.8%
Salary	28.0%
Combination of salary and productivity	24.4%
Hourly contract	15.9%
Percentage of full partner's wage	7.3%

Is income reduced if the physician doesn't take calls?

Yes	63.3%
No	36.7%

Is income reduced for not making hospital rounds?

Yes	37.0%
No	63.0%

Source: Medical Group Management Association, "Physicians–Part-Time or Partially Retired," *Information Exchange* #6566 (Englewood, CO: Medical Group Management Association, March 2006).

➤ How will compensation be handled? Will the current system accommodate the part-time schedule or will it be modified?

➤ How many calls is the physician willing to handle? If s/he won't be included in call coverage, will his or her compensation be reduced, and how will the call be shared among the other physicians?

➤ Will benefits, including vacation time, be reduced?

➤ What will be the policy in the future? Will part-time status be offered as a right if a physician meets certain criteria, such as years of service or age? Will it be offered only as a potential opportunity that physicians can request after achieving a certain age or number of service years, with the group determining if part-time status is possible or appropriate?

➤ Will there be a time limitation on part-time? The group can still elect to renew the status on a year-to-year basis, but the physician has no "right" to continue part-time status beyond what is agreed to.

➤ What will be the shareholder duties? You may determine that a part-time, senior physician's shareholder duties will cease on the date the part-time/slowdown status takes effect. A buyout arrangement would begin at the same time. This reflects that part-time physicians may have concerns and interests different from the other physicians, so they shouldn't have the same vote as full-time physicians.

➤ How will a physician who works part time affect your overhead calculations and staffing?

Sources:

Patricia J. Crome, "Part-Time Practice: An Exploratory Study to Define Preferred Models," ACMPE Professional Paper (Englewood, CO: American College of Medical Practice Executives, September 2001).

Lisa H. Schneck, "Know-How: Partly Problematic," *MGMA Connexion*, V. 2, No. 8, September 2002.

We'll have a new physician coming on board soon, and I need advice on developing the buy-in structure. What are recent trends related to practice buy-in, and how soon should we allow her to become a partner?

Many medical groups use practice buy-in approaches similar to those used in other professional service firms, where a new physician works as an associate for a defined period of time. This provides an opportunity to build a patient base

A CLOSER LOOK...

How many years must a physician work in the practice before s/he can buy in?

Practice type	Number of years	Number of responses
Primary care, including OB/GYN	1.45	20
Specialty	2.0	71
Multispecialty with primary and specialty	2.2	13

Source: Medical Group Management Association, "Buy-in and Buy-out Agreements," *Information Exchange* #6529 (Englewood, CO: Medical Group Management Association, January 2006).

---

while allowing the group's partner physicians to evaluate the associate's clinical competence and determine whether s/he should become an owner.

Owners expect physicians to meet certain targets related to revenue generation and clinical competence, as well as to maintain high-quality measures. They also often expect associates to provide a return on the practice's investment in hiring them. The returns do not have to be financial; they can relate to work shifted to the new physician or opportunities s/he creates for the practice.

Many arrangements require a new physician to meet buy-in obligations. One method increasingly used is a flat amount, usually $1,000 to $50,000. The trend is toward relatively small dollar amounts for both the buy-in and buyout. Two factors have contributed to this trend: (1) the lack of willingness on the part of graduating residents to participate in large buy-ins, and (2) the elimination of large buy-ins to relieve groups from making large payments to retiring physicians.

Groups should consider a buy-in amount that can be manageable for the new physician but large enough to ensure a long-term commitment to the group.

Another method to calculate buy-in is based on the value of the practice's hard assets and accounts receivable (A/R). A formula defines the purchase price of the "stock" – the depreciated book value of tangible assets, excluding A/R or goodwill, divided by the number of physicians who will be owners after the transaction. An additional value based on the A/R generated by the physician or a share of the total practice's A/R may also be defined and assessed.

The buy-in approach is influenced by the compensation model. A pure productivity-based model might require the partner to start from scratch in terms of generating A/R that will pay his or her compensation during the initial months as a partner or owner. Alternatively, the plan might provide credit for the A/R generated while the physician was an associate but not provide full credit for A/R in deferred-compensation arrangements paid over time after the physician leaves the practice.

Buyout arrangements reflect buy-in terms. In the flat-fee buy-in method, practices might return the buy-in amount when the physician departs. The same might apply to practices that use the stock-purchase method based on the value of hard assets. In the share-of-A/R method, the practice might pay the physician a portion of A/R via a deferred-compensation arrangement. The buy-in and buyout methods should be the same even though the dollar values might differ.

Sources:

Bruce A. Johnson, "Digest: The Bottom Line? Buy-in, Buy-out Arrangements Affect More Than That," *MGMA e-Connexion*, Issue 76, April 2005, www3.mgma.com/articles/index.cfm?fuseaction=detail.main&articleID=13344 (accessed August 10, 2006).

Hobart Collins. "Q & A: What is the Trend for Buy/Sell Agreements in Group Practices?" *MGMA e-Connexion*, Issue 19, November 2002, www3.mgma.com/articles/index.cfm?fuseaction=detail.main&articleID=12228 (accessed August 10, 2006).

QUESTION 50

How do I find data on employee salaries for medical practices?

The following sources provide information on medical staff salaries:

- MGMA local chapters (listed at www.mgma.com);
- Health Care Group's Staff Salary Survey (www.healthcaregroup.com);
- Professional Association of Health Care Office Management (www.pahcom.com);
- U.S. Department of Labor, Bureau of Labor Statistics, Wages by Area and Occupation (www.bls.gov/bls/blswage.htm); and
- Salary.com (www.salary.com).

QUESTION 51

Our practice is hiring a new physician. I need to renew our physician employment agreement and make sure it is up to date. What issues should I watch for in the agreement?

The employment agreement is the document stating what you expect out of the physician in terms of responsibilities and performance and what the physician can expect from the practice. Because of its importance in the relationship, you are wise to review the agreement on a regular basis.

The document should include the following items:

- A statement specifying the relationship between the practice (provide official name) and the physician. Is the physician an employee, associate, or partner?

Include another statement that the physician agrees to the relationship.

➤ The length of term of the agreement. The typical term is one year, but the agreement may include provisions for automatic renewal each year. Automatic renewals (often called evergreen provisions) eliminate the need to renegotiate the contract each year.

➤ Responsibilities of the physician, including treating patients, preparing charts, meeting attendance requirements, and keeping skills and knowledge current as specified by the state licensing board and specialty board. Include the practice's expectations for the work schedule and call coverage. You may also want to include specifics such as completing all dictations within 48 hours of the patient visit, and finishing all chart notes within 48 hours of the patient visit.

➤ Compensation plan or a referral to the group's compensation model. If the employment agreement automatically renews, be sure that the wording of the compensation statement allows for changes from year to year rather than locking in the compensation from the first year.

➤ Description of the space, supplies, and staff that the practice will provide to support the physician's responsibilities.

➤ Benefits offered by the practice, including vacation and sick leave; time off and allowance for continuing medical education; health, life, and disability insurance; retirement plan; automobile allowance; and allowance for professional membership dues and subscriptions.

➤ Malpractice insurance and indemnification. All physicians should receive the same insurance coverage based on their specialty and services. If the physician

FOR MORE INFORMATION...

Issues included or referred to in physician employment agreements covered in more detail in this book:

✔ Physician compensation plan, Question #52;

✔ Physician retirement and buyout, Question #40;

✔ Part-time schedules, Question #48;

✔ Partnership and buy-in agreements, Question #49;

✔ Inappropriate behavior and consequences, Question #53; and

✔ Physician code of conduct or ethics, and professional responsibility, Question #85.

---

is experienced, make sure that s/he is covered for incidents prior to the date of the agreement.

➤ Partnership opportunities and time frame.

➤ A statement that medical records are the property of the practice and stay with the practice if the physician leaves.

➤ Description of disability policy. Include a definition of disability, length of time allowed for disability, and if part-time employment after a disability will be allowed.

➤ Parameters for termination of the agreement. Some contracts state that the agreement may be terminated for any or no reason by providing written notice within 30 or 60 days. This may cause an alarm for the physician who may want to negotiate a longer notification period. Other contracts specify the actions that can cause termination, including:

- Loss of license;

- Lack of malpractice coverage;

- Suspension from any federal or private insurance program;

- Loss of privileges at a hospital;

- Conviction of a crime;

- Substance abuse addiction; or

- Behavior that threatens patient or staff safety.

➤ Noncompete covenants or nonsolicitation clauses. Noncompete statements describe the area in which the physician agrees not to practice after leaving your practice. State laws vary regarding applicability and how violations can be handled. Nonsolicitation clauses restrict the physician from soliciting patients, employees, and referral sources upon termination. Both should have time limits.

➤ Provision for arbitration. If disagreements develop over the terms of the contract, include a provision for arbitration as a less expensive alternative than legal suits.

➤ Assignment. Both parties agree that the agreement can't be assigned to another individual or organization without the other party's signature.

➤ Modification of agreement terms. You might want to add terms allowing for modification of provisions within the agreement, especially in areas regarding compensation, benefits, and responsibilities. Sample wording can be "modified by the employer at its sole discretion" or "subject to annual modification by the employer's board of directors." A wary physician may negotiate changes in the wording to require notification and consent of changes.

➤ Further assurances. Rather than specify the details of responsibilities of either party, the contract may include statements requiring each party to carry out the terms of the agreement. For instance, expecting the physician to provide all services necessary for comprehensive care and complete all forms and documents necessary to bill third-party payers. Sample wording of this provision is: "Each party hereto shall cooperate and take such action as may be reasonably requested by the other party in order to carry out the terms and purposes of this agreement and any other transactions contemplated herein."

As with all legal documents, reviewing employment agreements should be done with your group's legal counsel to ensure a full understanding of the terms and correct wording of modifications.

Sources:

Michael R. Burke, "Demystifying Common Terms in Employment Agreements," *Family Practice Management*, V. 10, No. 6, June 2003.

Steven Peltz, "Guidelines for Corporate Covenants and Physician Employment Agreements," *Journal of Medical Practice Management*, V. 19, No. 3, November/December 2003.

How can I develop a physician compensation model that physicians will be happy with and will maintain our productivity and revenue?

Physician compensation models are frequently reviewed and modified. Changes in the practice, in the group's income, in physicians' attitudes about its fairness, and a variety of other reasons lead to doubts that the current plan is the best plan. Because of the personal impact of the plan, physicians will be concerned about changes and should be involved in any revisions.

Compensation plans have two facets: the strictly financial aspect of the distribution of the group's income and ex-

A CLOSER LOOK...

Method used to determine compensation in better performing groups

100% production less allocated overhead	33.94%
50%-99% production less allocated overhead	15.60%
100% production-based share of compensation pool	7.34%
50%-99% production-based share of compensation pool	8.26%
100% equal share of compensation pool	8.26%
50%-99% base salary plus incentive	9.17%
100% straight/guaranteed salary	5.50%
Other	6.42%

Source: Medical Group Management Association, *Performance and Practices of Successful Medical Groups: 2005 Report Based on 2004 Data* (Englewood, CO: Medical Group Management Association, 2005).

Criteria for incentive-based compensation plans

	Percent of respondents
Productivity	92.7%
Patient satisfaction	7.3%
Quality of care	5.5%
Utilization rates	1.8%
Other criteria*	14.5%

* Other criteria included practice profit sharing, committee participation and leadership, professional and community presentations and activities, relative value units, seniority, and types of calls.

Source: Medical Group Management Association, "Income Distribution – Incentive Plans," *Information Exchange* #4890 (Englewood, CO: Medical Group Management Association, 2004).

---

penses and the cultural aspect. The latter dimension is often not considered, but how income is distributed affects the organizational culture (for example, its competitive, cooperative, and team-oriented nature), and so the plan should reflect the culture wanted in the organization.

A CLOSER LOOK...

What about pay for performance?

A relatively new issue in health care is the introduction of pay-for-performance programs. The general concept is that health plans and government payers compensate hospitals and physicians based on quality, utilization, and compliance with care standards rather than pay straight capitation or fee for service.

Measures used to base physician practice compensation include HbA1c management and control for diabetics, ventricular function assessment for congestive heart failure, and screenings and preventive care for breast cancer and colorectal cancer.

The concept is not widespread yet, but Medicare has begun a demonstration program. If pay-for-performance compensation becomes an increasing factor in your practice, the compensation plan will have to be adjusted to align its goals with that of the payers' programs.

Source: Lisa H. Schneck, "Quick Tip: Business Community Drives Health Care's Movement toward Pay for Performance," *MGMA e-Connexion*, Issue 88, November 2005.

The first step in revising the compensation plan is to review the practice's mission statements, core values, and vision. How does the practice see itself, what should its future be, and how does it get there? Without understanding these concepts, it is difficult to identify the organizational culture and develop a plan that supports the mission and vision.

Next, discuss what is wrong with the current compensation plan. Why does it need to be revised? Have there been changes in the practice (more physicians), practice financials (declining income), or demographics (trend toward pay-for-performance plans)? Do physicians feel that the plan is unfair and leads to unequal compensation? Is the current plan causing behavior counter to the organizational vision and culture? To get at the real issues, you may need to conduct individual interviews as well as group discussions.

If the discussions reveal concerns with minor issues, you may be able to revise the current plan rather than start a new one from scratch. If the major point of concern is declining income, you may also need to review the practice's financial statements. Are there ways of increasing efficiency, lowering operating costs, reducing accounts receivable, or generating additional revenue that will help with the issue?

With an understanding of the practice goals, culture, and current concerns, the next step is to determine the goals of the plan and how to reach those goals. There are general models that can be used based on the culture and goals. If the culture emphasizes individualism, the goal may be to increase individual production and reduce expenses. If a cooperative, team-based atmosphere is desired, the plan will encourage teamwork and shared effort in increasing revenue and decreasing expenses. Combinations of these plans are possible, such as basing compensation on a base salary plus productivity bonus.

The majority of medical practices use productivity-based plans; this is especially true of better performing groups. Production can be based on collections, gross charges, or physician work relative value units (RVUs). Even compensation plans based on a combination of base salary and incentives or bonuses may use production as the key factor in determining the bonus.

After a draft of the compensation model has been developed, present it to the group's physicians for review and comment. It may be impossible to please all of the physicians, but their objections should be heard and incorporated as much as possible. The group's leadership team should work with the physicians to address their concerns and discuss the limitations of the plan. When a draft has been agreed upon, conduct a vote to approve the plan as final.

FOR MORE INFORMATION . . .

Additional resources from MGMA for physician compensation models:

✔ *Physician Compensation Plans: State-of-the-Art Strategies,* by Bruce A. Johnson, JD, MPA, and Deborah L. Walker, PhD, FACMPE, 2006.

✔ *Physician Compensation: Models for Aligning Financial Goals and Incentives,* 2nd Edition, by Kenneth M. Hekman, FACMPE, 2002.

✔ "Income Distribution – Academic Practice," *Information Exchange* #5986, 2003.

✔ "Income Distribution – Expense Allocation," *Information Exchange* #4294, 2003.

✔ "Income Distribution – Relative Value Units (RVUs)," *Information Exchange* #5137, 2006.

Sources:

Will N. Ginn, "10 Considerations for a Successful Physician Compensation Plan," *MGMA Connexion,* V. 5, No. 8, September 2005.

Bruce A. Johnson, "Quick Tip: When Revising Physician Compensation Plans, Know the Old Before Starting the New," *MGMA e-Connexion,* Issue 89, November 2005.

QUESTION 53

How should I deal with a physician who displays inappropriate behavior?

Physicians may behave inappropriately for a variety of reasons. Your first action should be to identify and document the objectionable behavior. Make sure that the behavior is disruptive to the practice and not just a case of an employee having a personal conflict with the physician. It is important to separate personal issues from those that are not. If the behavior is truly inappropriate or goes against the practice's culture, you should approach the physician with sensitivity and tact to identify the cause of the behavior. The cause will determine the appropriate action. You should be certain that you have specific events or actions clearly documented to share with the physician.

Your practice should have formal policies on how inappropriate behavior and substance abuse are addressed. Formal policies ensure a standard approach and minimize the interference of personal bias. The practice administrator or executive typically leads and is in charge of the issue, but physician leadership should also be involved when the behavior of physicians must be addressed. The physician leader and administrator should be involved jointly in meetings and resolutions related to the issue.

Use the three-step approach (see "A Closer Look" on the next page) to address the issue, understand the physician's side, and discuss resolutions. Use the policies, physician's employment agreement, code of ethics, or other practice documents to support your position. Discuss what behavior needs to be changed and what disciplinary action may be taken if no changes occur. Disciplinary action can include mandatory counseling, treatment programs, written reprimands, and, eventually, termination. Offer options such as counseling prior to discipline, if possible.

If the inappropriate behavior is caused by substance abuse, a quicker, stronger response may be necessary to protect patient safety. The physician may be expected to enter a treatment program or face termination. With issues related to substance abuse, you should seek the advice of your legal counsel or a human resources attorney to ensure that proper procedures are followed.

Prevention is always a better tactic than waiting for an incident to develop. Your practice's policies regarding inappropriate behavior and substance abuse should be made clear during the recruitment process. Watch for signs of

A CLOSER LOOK...

The following is a three-step approach toward data gathering and conflict resolution:

1. Ask questions to learn each party's viewpoint and listen. Don't interject your own view; rather, just clarify each side.
2. Ask "Is there anything else I should know about this?" Let the person know you've heard and understand. State that you want some time to think about the issue and suggest another time to meet.
3. At the next meeting, reiterate what you understand to be the issue and suggest a solution. In the following discussion, use mostly questions, rather than statements, to respond to objections.

Source: Marshall Colt, "Know-How: Managing the Difficult Doc," *MGMA Connexion*, V. 5, No. 9, October 2005.

---

low morale, burnout, and behavioral changes that should be addressed early. Make sure physicians and employees are aware of employee assistance programs or other resources.

If you address behavioral problems early and appropriately, you can bring about changes for the benefit of the individual and the practice, while minimizing disruption and discipline. Make sure that your practice has policies in place related to the practice's response to inappropriate behavior and substance abuse.

Sources:

Hobart Collins, "The Problem Physician," *Directions Newsletter*, V. 4, No. 4, 2002.

Amy L. Wray Irish, "Crunching Numbers: Guidance for Disciplining a Problem Physician," *MGMA e-Connexion*, February 2004.

Medical Group Management Association, "Physicians – Discipline," *Information Exchange* #3091 (Englewood, CO: Medical Group Management Association, 2003).

Bergitta E. Smith, "Does an Impaired Clinician Threaten Your Practice?" *MGMA Connexion*, V. 4, No. 6, July 2004.

QUESTION 54

I'd like to change our employee performance appraisal process. Do you have advice on developing one that is equitable and encourages high performance levels?

Employee performance reviews are important to an organization's success, not only as a way of reviewing employees' past performance, but also to encourage excellence in future performance and alignment with organizational goals. Performance assessments often fail to produce desired outcomes if the performance items seem irrelevant, outdated, or out of line with the goals and mission of the organization. The criteria for rating performance must be both behavioral and performance based and applied equitably. The review process does not encourage improved performance if there are not appropriate incentives or consequences.

If you want to implement a more successful performance appraisal process, start with your group's mission, vision, and goals. Employee performance goals should be aligned with the goals and strategies of the organization. If the group's goal is to improve customer service and patient satisfaction, then each performance review should incorporate customer service and patient satisfaction.

Performance reviews are often based on standard criteria such as job knowledge, quality, efficiency or productivity, teamwork, and customer satisfaction. Supervisors and employees should meet at the beginning of each calendar or fiscal year to review the job description and use it to discuss performance goals and the review process. Quarterly or midyear meetings should be used to address performance concerns to provide opportunities to improve performance before the end of the year.

At the end of the year, supervisors should prepare for performance review meetings by carefully assessing each employee's performance throughout the entire year and

A CLOSER LOOK...

Practice Adds Peer Review to Performance Appraisal Process

Employees at West Shore Urology PC in Muskegon, Mich., were unhappy with the performance evaluation process. Managers realized that teamwork needed to be reinforced. During an off-site retreat, the staff developed a peer review process whereby employees evaluate other employees they work with. Ratings were based on teamwork, versatility, responsiveness, and other factors. Managers reviewed comments to discourage negative criticism. Peer review determined 10 percent of the total review.

Employees are pleased with the system because it increases awareness of how their actions affect others. Managers like the additional input and have noticed the increased cohesiveness of the organization.

Source: Ariana Harner, "Quick Tip: Case Study: Employee Performance Appraisal and Merit Bonus Incentive," *MGMA e-Connexion*, Issue 20, November 2002.

---

framing their concerns into constructive feedback. Keys to a successful performance review include:

➤ Evaluating the employee based on full performance rather than on just one event;

➤ Basing appraisals on objective data rather than hearsay or personal preferences;

➤ Evaluating each trait individually rather than letting one trait bias the evaluation of another criterion;

➤ Providing a completed review prior to the meeting to allow the employee time to reflect on it;

➤ Allowing time to discuss the rating, including where performance has been excellent;

- Being open minded, showing empathy, and listening to what the employee is saying;

- Providing constructive feedback and reasonable suggestions for improvement in areas that need it; and

- Not letting the review process get personal. The topic is work performance, not personality issues.

Employee performance appraisals will not be effective if no rewards, incentives, or consequences are tied to performance evaluations. Merit increases are often based on results. For example, employees with overall ratings of "Excellent" or "Exceeding Expectations" may receive a 4 percent raise, whereas those receiving "Good" or "Meeting Expectations" may receive a 2 percent increase. Poor evaluations may result in progressive discipline and eventually termination, but it is better not to wait until the end of the year for giving feedback to the poorest performers.

There are additional concepts that you can incorporate into your review process to improve it:

- **Employee self-evaluations** – Employees evaluate their own performance before meeting with their supervisor. Disparities between employee and supervisor are discussed to understand how expectations and perspectives differ.

- **Goal-setting appraisals** – At the beginning of the year, supervisors and employees identify the year's performance goals aligned with the job descriptions and the organizational goals. Developing the goals together strengthens employee commitment to the process. This option works well for managerial positions.

- **Competency-based reviews** – Employees are evaluated on the additional skills and knowledge they acquire to the benefit of the organization. Supervisors

FOR MORE INFORMATION . . .

Performance appraisal resources:

- ✔ *Medical Performance Management Manual: How to Evaluate Employees,* 2nd Edition, by Courtney Price and Alys Novak (Englewood, CO: Medical Group Management Association, 2001).
- ✔ "Employee Performance Appraisals," *Information Exchange* #4237 (Englewood, CO: Medical Group Management Association, 2005).
- ✔ "Employee Incentive Plans," *Information Exchange* #4880 (Englewood, CO: Medical Group Management Association).

---

and employees must identify new skills or knowledge and be able to commit time and resources to education and opportunities. These reviews are based on the competencies and skills needed to successfully perform the duties assigned.

➤ **360-degree feedback** – Individuals are evaluated by peers, supervisors, and/or subordinates. This option may be especially valuable for managers, supervisors, and physicians. Consider the influence of bias and whether or not evaluations should be anonymous.

Performance reviews done properly can be time consuming. However, the payback is that employee performance is aligned with organizational goals and employees are more motivated.

Sources:

Ashish Chandra, "Employee Evaluation Strategies for Healthcare Organizations – A General Guide," *Hospital Topics,* V. 84, No. 2, Spring 2006.

Michael A. O'Connell and Deborah M. Jewell, "Human Resources Management in Group Practice," in *Physician Practice Management: Essential Operational and Financial Knowledge,* ed. Lawrence F. Wolper (Sudbury, MA: Jones and Bartlett Publishers, 2005).

Courtney Price and Bruce Stickler, "Performance Management and Planning for the 21st Century," *Personnel Postscript/HR Issues,* V. 15, No. 2, February 2000.

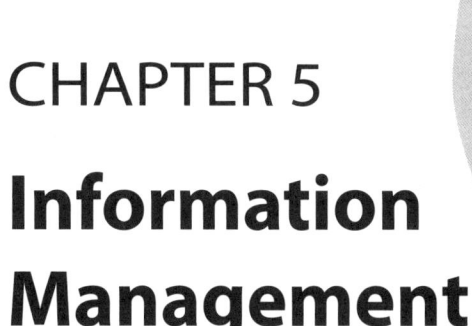

CHAPTER 5

Information Management

QUESTION 55

What process should I use to select a practice management system?

Selecting a new system that is the best available option for your group requires several steps and involves many participants. The recommended steps in the selection process are:

1. Conduct a needs assessment to determine the functions the system must include. Answering the following questions will help you in your assessment:

    ➢ What functions are needed to support your long-term goals?

    ➢ What are the limits of your current system?

    ➢ What functions do you wish your current system had?

    ➢ What inefficiencies or limitations do you have in your practice currently, and what do you hope to accomplish with an electronic medical record (EMR)?

    ➢ Are missing charts a problem? How much time is spent seeking "misplaced" charts? Are lab reports and test results in the chart or "missing in action"?

    ➢ Are provider notes difficult to read?

    ➢ Are providers interested in electronic prescribing?

    ➢ Do you want to be able to print individualized patient education information before the patient leaves the exam room?

- Do you play telephone tag with patients because staff doesn't have ready access to needed information?

- Is patient e-mail or Web access a future goal?

2. Involve the employees and physicians who will be using the new system. Ask them about their needs and ideas. Record what functions the system must have and what functions you'd like it to have.

3. Develop and distribute a request for proposal (RFP) based on the needs assessment and your group's characteristics. Identify vendors to receive your RFP by talking to colleagues, attending technology meetings, and looking at vendor Websites. (See Question #57 for information on developing RFPs.)

4. Interview vendors based on their response to the RFP. Remember, the EMR system you purchase this year needs to be the EMR system you're still using in five or 10 years. The company selected should be one you trust. Does its off-the-shelf product include the must-have items on your list, or will it have to be customized? Discuss the support, implementation assistance, and training it offers. How many installations have they handled? How will the system integrate with your EHR, accounting, or other programs?

5. View a demonstration of the program and ask for hands-on time with it; don't just watch the demonstrator go through the motions. Include representatives from all departments who will be using the system. Develop evaluation sheets for the participants to rate the vendors on ease of use.

6. Ask for and contact references. Ask these reference practices if the vendor carried out its promises, if the program met their expectations, and what problems or issues they encountered with the system.

CHAPTER 5: Information Management 151

Reference practices should have similar characteristics to yours, if possible.

7. Investigate the financial health of the vendor and parent firm of the system (if not the vendor).

8. Negotiate the price and contract terms, including payment terms, training, and ongoing support.

Sources:

Cynthia Dunn, "Quick Tip: Byte the Technology Bullet – IT Possibilities, Challenges and Resources," *MGMA e-Connexion,* Issue 87, October 2005.

"Shopping for an EHR Contract," *Medical Economics Infotech Bulletin,* October 4, 2005, www.memag.com/memag/article/articleDetail.jsp?id=184288&searchString =RFP (accessed August 20, 2006).

QUESTION 56

How can I implement the use of handheld computers and personal digital assistants in our clinical practice?

Personal digital assistants (PDAs) have many practical uses in medical practices and can lead to increased efficiencies, improved charge capture, and enhanced patient safety.

Applications for handheld devices include:

➤ **Charge capture** – With encounter forms loaded on the PDA, it is easy for physicians to complete the form for each encounter and upload the information into the practice management system at day's end. PDAs are especially effective for capturing off-site visits to hospitals and nursing homes. Coding aids can also be added, improving the accuracy and efficiency of the coding and billing process. One medical center realized a substantial reduction in coding and billing staff after a PDA-based charge capture system was implemented.

➤ **Patient care** – Reference resources that provide assistance in clinical decision making can be loaded

A CLOSER LOOK...

Tablet Case Study

Shawnee Mission Physicians Group and the Shawnee Mission Medical Center developed a PC tablet-based charge capture system. Its features include:

- ✔ Daily patient lists that are updated as patients are admitted;
- ✔ New patient information form preloaded with ICD-9 codes;
- ✔ Diagnosis and procedure information;
- ✔ Medication notes; and
- ✔ Discharge summary information.

The tablets use a wireless connection to the main hospital system for seamless transmission of data for billing and patient care.

Source: Leslie R. Jebson, Christopher Shireman, and Gregory T. Sweat, "Tablet Makes for Good Medicine: Case Study: Tablet-style Computer Enhances Physician Satisfaction, Revenue Stream," *MGMA Connexion*, V. 5, No. 10, November 2005.

---

on PDAs, providing easy access regardless of the physician's location.

➤ **Prescriptions** – Prescription management programs provide information on drug formularies, recommended dosages, and interactions. PDAs can be linked to pharmacies for electronic prescriptions or used to print the prescription, which eliminates the problem of illegible handwriting.

➤ **Time management tools** – PDAs are frequently used for managing calendars, schedules, phone and address lists, and e-mail, saving time and increasing efficiency.

CHAPTER 5: Information Management

PDAs should be set up to require a password for accessing patient information and to log off automatically after use; this process meets the security and privacy regulations of the Health Insurance Portability and Accountability Act (HIPAA).

As beneficial as PDAs are in medical groups, they are not miracle workers. Physicians must remember to keep them charged and, at times, can "forget" where they put them. If you have physicians who currently forget to check their schedules or complete their encounter forms, there is no guarantee that the PDA will help them remember.

Sources:

Michael G. McElroy, "Automation and Technology Resources for Small Medical Groups," *MGMA Connexion*, V. 5, No. 8, September 2005.

Rosemarie Nelson, "Academic Practices and Technology," *APA Matrix*, V. 18, No. 4, September 2004.

Elizabeth Woodcock, *Mastering Patient Flow: More Ideas to Increase Efficiency and Earnings*, 2nd Edition (Englewood, CO: Medical Group Management Association, 2003).

QUESTION 57

Should I use an RFP for the purchase of a new computer system? What are some hints for developing one?

Developing a request for proposal (RFP) can be a time-consuming process, leading some managers to question the value of this step. It may seem easier to have many vendors come to the practice and demonstrate their products. One advantage of the RFP, however, is that it requires the end user to thoroughly analyze the goals of purchasing the new system and the functions that are needed. This analysis allows you to target those vendors that match your needs and qualifications. Having a structured basis for evaluating each vendor's products will result in a better match for your group's needs.

FOR MORE INFORMATION...

Additional resource

✔ MGMA's *Information Exchange* #4879, "Information Systems Selection – RFIs and RFPs," provides several sample RFPs from various medical practices.

It is not necessary to send out more than six RFPs. Evaluating the returned information is time consuming. By limiting the number of RFPs, the process becomes more manageable.

The RFP should be developed only after you have conducted a thorough needs assessment (see Question #55). The resulting detailed understanding of the organizational goals and system requirements will provide the specifics needed to write the RFP.

Include in the RFP:

➤ An overview describing the purpose of the RFP;

➤ Contact information;

➤ The timeline for the selection process, including the proposal due date, expected time frame for demonstrations, and the target selection date;

➤ Information on how to respond to the RFP (such as how many paper copies to send or how to respond electronically);

➤ Vendor information wanted in the proposals, including the vendor's capabilities related to specific requirements; the vendor's history, financial information, and number of installations; and customer references;

- ➤ A detailed list of system requirements and additional features;

- ➤ Training and implementation support services required;

- ➤ Cost specifications; and

- ➤ Terms and conditions.

The RFP should ask vendors to:

- ➤ List and provide pricing for all hardware and software components;

- ➤ Break out training and support costs;

- ➤ Describe how the system integrates with your current programs;

- ➤ Address HIPAA requirements;

- ➤ Include a return-on-investment (ROI) calculation based on their products' features and modules that you've selected; and

- ➤ Provide a detailed implementation process with a reasonable timeline.

Sources:

Margret Amatayakul and Steven S. Lazarus, *Electronic Health Records: Transforming Your Medical Practice* (Englewood, CO: Medical Group Management Association, 2005).

Cynthia Dunn, "Quick Tip: Byte the Technology Bullet – IT Possibilities, Challenges and Resources," *MGMA e-Connexion,* Issue 87, October 2005.

Beckie Kelly Schuerenberg, "Some CIOs Tired of Making the Same Old Requests," *Health Data Management,* V. 12, No. 2, February 2004, www.healthdatamanagement.com/html/current/CurrentIssueStory.cfm?PostID=16922 (accessed February 24, 2004).

QUESTION 58

I need to develop a policy for IT issues in the group, such as security, Internet usage, and e-mail usage. What should I include in it? Are samples available?

All practices should have policies addressing employee use of business computers for personal use. Employees' misuse of computers could result in distractions from work, accessing inappropriate information for the workplace, and security breaches affecting the groups' network.

Policies should include the following statements:

➤ Employees shall not download programs onto computers or the groups' network without the express permission of the information technology department;

➤ Employees shall not play computer games or access the Internet for personal use during work time;

➤ Employees shall not use the business computers and network to access, download, post, or share information or items that are discriminatory, sexually inappropriate, violent, or otherwise unacceptable in the workplace;

➤ Employees shall not use the group's information system for an outside business or to engage in illegal activity;

➤ Employees shall not attempt to access the information system using passwords or routes other than those assigned to them; and

➤ Violation of any of these policies shall be cause for disciplinary action, including termination.

The following sample policy is from MGMA's *Operating Policies & Procedures Manual for Medical Practices*, 3rd Edition:

Computer and Internet Policy

This document formalizes the policy for employees of [The Practice] on the use of **information technology resources**; including computers, printers and other peripherals, programs, data, local and wide area networks, and the Internet.

1. User Responsibilities

It is the responsibility of all employees of [The Practice] to read, understand, and follow this policy. In addition, users are expected to exercise reasonable judgment in interpreting this policy. Any person with questions regarding the application or meaning of this policy should seek clarification from appropriate management. Failure to observe this policy may subject individuals to disciplinary action, including termination of employment.

2. Unacceptable Uses of the Computer

Unless such use is reasonably related to a user's job, it is unacceptable for any person to use [The Practice's] computers:

- in furtherance of any illegal act, including violation of any criminal or civil laws or regulations, whether state or federal;
- for any political purpose;
- for any commercial purpose;
- to send threatening or harassing messages, whether sexual or otherwise;
- to access or share sexually explicit, obscene, or otherwise inappropriate materials;
- to infringe any intellectual property rights;
- to gain, or attempt to gain, unauthorized access to any computer or network;
- for any use that causes interference with or disruption of network users and resources, including propagation of computer viruses or other harmful programs;
- to intercept communications intended for other persons;
- to misrepresent either [The Practice] or a person's role at [The Practice];
- to distribute chain letters;
- to access any games site (solitaire, free cell, etc.);
- to access online gambling sites;

- to libel or otherwise defame any person; or
- for any personal use (except during break or lunch times), including instant messaging, chat rooms, etc.

3. Data Confidentiality

In the course of performing their jobs, [The Practice's] employees often have access to confidential or proprietary information, such as personal data about identifiable individuals or commercial information about business organizations. Under no circumstances is it permissible for employees to acquire access to confidential data unless such access is required by their jobs. Under no circumstances may employees disseminate any confidential information that they have rightful access to, unless such dissemination is required by their jobs.

4. Copyright Protection

Computer programs are valuable intellectual property. Software publishers can be very aggressive in protecting their property rights from infringement. In addition to software, legal protections can also exist for any information published on the Internet, such as the text and graphics on a Website. As such, it is important that users respect the rights of intellectual property owners. Users should exercise care and judgment when copying or distributing computer programs or information that could reasonably be expected to be copyrighted.

5. Computer Viruses

Users should exercise reasonable precautions in order to prevent the introduction of a computer virus into the local area or wide area networks. Virus scanning software is used to check any software downloaded from the Internet or obtained from any questionable source. Virus scanning software may not provide 100 percent protection; therefore, files or attachments from unknown or questionable sources should not be opened. In addition, executable files (program files that end in ".exe") and downloaded files should not be stored on or run from network drives.

6. Network Security

Our desktop computers are connected to a local area network, which links computers within [The Practice]. As such, it is critically important that users take particular care to avoid compromising the security of the network. Most importantly, users should never share their passwords with anyone else, and should promptly notify [The Practice] Information Technology personnel if they suspect their passwords have been compromised. In addition, users who will be leaving their

PCs unattended for extended periods should either log off the network or have a password-protected screen saver in operation. **No user is allowed to access the Internet or other external networks via modem unless their Internet activities are directly related to their job. It is permissible to use the Internet during your personal break and lunch times; however, all rules as outlined apply.**

7. E-mail

When using e-mail, there are several points users should consider. First, because e-mail addresses identify the organization that sent the message, users should consider e-mail messages to be the equivalent of letters sent on official letterhead. For the same reason, users should ensure that all e-mails are written in a professional and courteous tone. Finally, although many users regard e-mail as being like a telephone in offering a quick, informal way to communicate, users should remember that e-mails can be stored, copied, printed, or forwarded by recipients. As such, users should not write anything in an e-mail message that they would not feel just as comfortable putting into a memorandum.

8. No Expectation of Privacy

All computers are the property of [The Practice] and are to be used in conformance with this policy. [The Practice] retains, and when reasonable and in pursuit of legitimate needs for supervision, control, and the efficient and proper operation of the workplace, [The Practice] will exercise the right to inspect any user's computer, any data contained in it, and any data sent or received by that computer. Users should be aware that network administrators, in order to ensure proper network operations, routinely monitor network traffic. Use of the computers at [The Practice] constitutes express consent for [The Practice] to monitor and/or inspect any data that users create or receive, any messages they send or receive, and any Websites that they access.

_____   _____
Employee Signature   Date

_____
Employee Printed Name

FOR MORE INFORMATION...

The following sources contain sample policies and guidelines related to information technology use:

✔ Elizabeth Woodcock and Bette Warn, *Operating Policies & Procedures Manual for Medical Practices*, 3rd Edition (Englewood, CO: Medical Group Management Association, 2006).

✔ Courtney Price and Alys Novak, *HR Policies & Procedures Manual for Medical Practices*, 4th Edition (Englewood, CO: Medical Group Management Association, 2007).

QUESTION 59

I need to conduct an ROI analysis for purchasing an electronic health record (EHR) system. What advice and resources do you have to help me?

A return-on-investment (ROI) analysis of electronic health records is a thorough analysis of the benefits of implementing the system compared with the initial and ongoing costs. The ROI should be a major factor in deciding whether or not to purchase the system. EHR vendors often provide ROIs for their systems. Use this information with caution, however, because they will emphasize only the benefits.

The foreseen benefits should include operational efficiencies as well as financial benefits. Whenever possible, the benefits should be quantifiable and not just anecdotal. This may require a detailed time and cost analysis of current operations and issues. For example, state that complete medical records will be accessible in the exam room 100 percent of the time instead of the current X percent, and there will be X hours saved by not looking for the missing record or test result.

Not all benefits can be directly traced to cost savings or increased revenue, but they should still be recorded. Benefits may include a reduction in medical errors, improved status in negotiating with health plans, increased patient satisfaction, and a reduction in the potential for malpractice suits, which may result in lower malpractice premiums.

Develop a template that tabulates the benefit categories, the quantifiable benefits, and the time frame to realize the benefits. Quantifiable benefits include, for example, that charts are available in exam rooms 100 percent of the time, and pulling a paper chart saves X minutes per day vs. accessing an electronic record. Some benefits may not be immediate because of the time required to fully implement all of the features.

Margret Amatayakul, coauthor of *Electronic Health Records: Transforming Your Medical Practice,* recommends the following benefit categories for EHRs:

➤ Record accessibility;

➤ Provider productivity;

➤ Operational savings;

➤ Information quality;

➤ Patient satisfaction;

➤ Patient safety;

➤ Outcomes; and

➤ Cost of care.

Track the costs of the current system, itemizing all costs related to the management of paper records. In your cost chart, track your current costs, how the EHR will change the costs, and note your assumptions about the changes. Current costs include:

A CLOSER LOOK...

EHR Success Story

John J. Masiello, CMPE, administrator and COO of Bergen Medical Alliance, says that their group optimized practice efficiencies after their EHR system was implemented.

"Between increased physician productivity, billing revenue, and reduced expenses, we calculated that in our EHR's first year, our return on investment averaged $23 per patient visit per year — or a net gain of $56,652 per physician per year."

Source: Christina Pope, "Defining the Profession: Win the Technology Marathon," *MGMA Connexion*, V. 4, No. 4, April 2004.

➤ Paper chart supplies (such as folders, paper, and tabs);

➤ Transcription costs;

➤ Storage expenses;

➤ Archival storage rental costs;

➤ Records of staff salary and benefits;

➤ Malpractice premiums (compared to a possible discount if an EHR system is implemented); and

➤ Uncaptured charges.

The next step is to outline and calculate the total costs of purchasing and implementing the EHR system. You will need to obtain the specific costs from the EHR vendors with which you are negotiating. Make sure you have thoroughly discussed the total costs so that there will be no surprises with the final contract. A cost worksheet will include columns for assumptions, initial and annual costs, and ongoing costs.

The following examples of cost elements are suggested by Margret Amatayakul:

- ➤ Hardware (list servers, storage devices and media, telecom devices, etc.);

- ➤ Software (EHR package, operating system, upgrades, etc.);

- ➤ Selection support (consultant, conferences, etc.);

- ➤ Implementation and training (training costs, loss of revenue during implementation, consultants, data conversion, etc.); and

- ➤ Maintenance (hardware service, software license, telecom fees, etc.).

It is important to analyze all of the potential costs, including data conversion from the current system, ongoing maintenance costs, costs related to selecting the system and receiving training, and costs of reduced productivity during the implementation and learning phase.

The final step in the ROI analysis is to compare the savings from all of the benefits with the total costs, and trending the benefits and costs for several years. It may take several years to realize cost savings; however, the savings related to efficiency should appear soon after implementation.

Sources:

Margret Amatayakul and Steven S. Lazarus, *Electronic Health Records: Transforming Your Medical Practice* (Englewood, CO: Medical Group Management Association, 2005).

David N. Gans, "Tech Talk: Techno-Smarts: Tools to Calculate ROI for Technology Purposes," *MGMA Connexion*, V. 5, No. 4, April 2005.

FOR MORE INFORMATION . . .

Another ROI analysis tool available from the Medical Group Management Association is the IT Return on Investment Calculator (in Microsoft® Excel).

To access this tool, go to the Member area of the MGMA Website (www.mgma.com) and select Tools.

QUESTION 60

How do I convince my physician owners that a new IT system is necessary?

Physicians will respond to your request if presented with enough data and education on the benefits of a new system. Conduct a return on investment (ROI) analysis to provide the cost benefits of purchasing a new system (see Question #59 for information on ROI assessments). Patient acceptance of an electronic medical record (EMR) system is high. Consumer familiarity with and confidence in information technology is strong, regardless of the consumer's age and nationality.

Educate the physicians at every opportunity. There are many providers using EMR systems that have seen benefits such as streamlining office workflow, creating more complete documentation, improving patient care, reducing errors, increasing patient satisfaction, and reducing costs associated with traditional transcription. As issues or questions arise, explain the limitations of the current system and how a new system would provide you with additional information, accomplish additional tasks, increase efficiencies, and provide savings that lead to increased revenue and compensation.

You may have one or more physicians within the group who agree with you or who can be convinced. Encourage them to take up your cause and advocate the benefits of a new system to other physicians.

Some physicians may disagree with having a new EMR system because of their skepticism toward information technology or a fear of change. They will need reassurance and more details on ease of use and benefits. Your physician champion may be able to help.

Discuss options for paying for the new system. The physicians may be concerned that their compensation will be reduced. Is outsourcing an option? The ROI analysis documents the planned long-term savings, but what about savings in the short term?

Provide data analyzing better performing groups' success with electronic health record (EHR) technology. Multispecialty groups with EHR systems report 17 percent higher total physician compensation and benefits per full-time-equivalent (FTE) physician than practices without EHR, according to data from the 2004 MGMA Successful Groups Cost Survey Supplement. Those practices spent 70 percent more on information technology than groups without an EHR system, but they reported substantially greater total medical revenue, which more than offset the higher operating costs. The net result was this: Physicians in those practices had a median personal income of $285,239, an amount $41,905 greater than the physicians in practices without an EHR system.

Practices that spend less than $7,000 per FTE physician have substantially lower revenues, operating costs, and profit than practices that spend more on IT. In virtually every specialty, the practices that spend the most on IT (more than $20,000 per FTE physician) have the most profit. The profit for multispecialty groups that spent more than $7,000 on IT was 42 percent greater than the practices that spent less than $7,000.

Providing physicians with ROI data, educating them about current limitations and future capabilities, and letting them hear from your physician champion should eventually bring them around to the knowledge that the investment is necessary and worthwhile.

Sources:

David N. Gans, "On the Edge: Does Technology Pay? (Yes)," *MGMA Connexion*, V. 5, No. 6, July 2005.

Christina Pope, "Defining the Profession: Win the Technology Marathon," *MGMA Connexion*, V. 4, No. 4, April 2004.

QUESTION 61

How can I stay up to date on the latest technologies for group practices?

Practice administrators are overwhelmed with daily responsibilities and have little time to keep current on recent information technology (IT) advances. However, the increasing role of technology requires you to be aware of new advances affecting health care and improving practice administration.

A variety of resources exist to inform practice administrators on IT applications. Most professional associations' conferences include seminars on information technology and exhibit halls filled with IT vendors. Watch for additional education opportunities, like audio or Web-based seminars. Many Internet sites, magazines, and journals include articles and directories of vendors and their products. Opportunities to learn from your peers include participating in online discussion forums and bringing up the topic at meetings. Consultants can provide assistance when application selection and vendor evaluation appear overwhelming.

Health care IT resources include the following:

- Professional associations and their Websites:
    - Medical Group Management Association, www.mgma.com. Look at the MGMA Information Management Society online discussion group and other resources.
    - Healthcare Information and Management Systems Society, www.himss.org. HIMSS focuses on providing leadership for the optimal use of health care IT and management systems for the betterment of human health.

CHAPTER 5: Information Management

- Internet sites:
  - Healthcare IT Yellow Pages, www.health-infosys-dir.com/yp_hc.asp.
- Magazines and journals and their Websites:
  - *Advance for Health Information Executives,* health-care-it.advanceweb.com.
  - *Health Data Management,* www.healthdatamanagement.com.
  - *Health Management Technology,* www.healthmgttech.com.
  - *Healthcare Informatics,* www.healthcare-informatics.com.

Do I need to back up my data at an off-site storage location?

Off-site storage is recommended because any number of disasters can destroy your backup that is stored on site. Although you may feel your location is safe from hurricanes, floods, or other natural disasters, many other disasters, such as broken pipes and fires, could strike at any location and at any time.

The traditional method for backing up data is to physically transport backup tapes or other media to an off-site storage facility. This system is awkward and may result in delays in obtaining the storage media from the location or even the destruction of the backup media. Today, better options include backing up data to remote facilities over the Internet. The system can be automated to ensure regular backups.

The HIPAA Standards for Electronic Security require data backup, although the standards do not specify the location of the backup. HIPAA requires contingency plans for each health care organization that include a data-backup plan to ensure recovery of information. Disaster recovery plans describing the restoration of systems and data are also required. Each organization is required to develop media controls regarding the transfer of data-containing media in and out of your facility, including media used for data backup.

If vendors are used for off-site storage, HIPAA requires a business associate contract with the vendor agreeing to:

- Implement administrative, physical, and technical safeguards that protect the confidentiality and integrity of the electronic protected health information (PHI);

- Ensure that any subcontractor agrees to implement the equivalent safeguards;

- Report any security incident; and

- Terminate the contract if the practice determines that the vendor has violated the terms of the contract.

Regardless of HIPAA, we still recommend these steps to ensuring data security. The benefits of off-site storage outweigh the disadvantages, especially when an automated process is in place.

Sources:

David Koeller, "Tech Talk: Save Yourself! The Importance of Disaster Recovery," *MGMA Connexion*, V. 5, No. 2, February 2005.

Robert M. Tennant and Aaron N. Krupp, *HIPAA Toolbox, Tool 4, Standards for Electronic Security* (Englewood, CO: Medical Group Management Association, 2004).

QUESTION 63

Should I hire information technology (IT) staff or use an outsourced model to meet my IT needs?

Medical practices frequently choose to outsource all or some of their IT functions because of the perceived benefits. You should look closely at the advantages and disadvantages of application service providers (ASPs) and other vendors prior to committing. Ask yourself, why are we thinking of outsourcing? If it is just for system cost savings, you may be disappointed. If it is to gain operational efficiencies and to expand system capabilities, along with cost savings, you may be satisfied.

Benefits of outsourcing IT functions include:

➤ Expertise of contractor's employees;

➤ Cost savings in salary and benefits for the IT positions;

➤ Reduced costs compared to purchasing hardware and software;

➤ Increased time for the group's employees to concentrate on other issues; and

➤ Service improvement by maximizing system capabilities and performance.

Small practices especially benefit when outsourcing enables the use of a more complex system and a high level of IT expertise than they could otherwise afford. Other practices also benefit when there is a tight market for IT personnel, current IT costs are well above other practices, or a current IT operation is not providing the service that is needed. Outsourcing can free the IT department for strategic development rather than handling everyday system issues.

Several concerns related to outsourcing that need to be carefully evaluated are the following:

➤ How long will the contractor be around? What is its financial health?

➤ Will the contractor provide the service and response that you need?

➤ Will the contracted IT employee be more loyal to your practice or to his or her employer?

➤ Will there be ongoing cost savings? Contractors need to make their profit, too. Some practices have found that savings only occur in the first year or two.

➤ Can issues related to the lack of knowledge or expertise among IT staff be overcome with additional training?

➤ Is data integrity and security an issue with outsourcing? What security measures do the vendors have in place? Are they HIPAA compliant?

Additional factors to consider as part of the decision-making process include the following:

➤ Will all IT functions be outsourced or only one or two? For example, you can outsource the EHR but keep remaining functions in house. Make sure the EHR system can integrate with the current systems.

➤ What legal advisors and consultants should be brought in? You may need help negotiating the maze of vendors and their offers. Contracts should always be reviewed by your legal counsel.

➤ What measures for level of service or performance will be used? If the vendor fails to meet project deadlines or service measures, what are the penalties?

CHAPTER 5: Information Management

You must seriously weigh the pros and cons of outsourcing any function. Information technology is an increasingly complex but increasingly important function within medical practices. Networking with your peers will help in understanding how outsourcing has succeeded or not in other practices. Your practice is unique, however, and your decisions for outsourcing are specific to it, so the decision must be based on what is right for your practice.

Sources:

Vince Ciotti and Bob Pagnotta, "The Other Side of Outsourcing," *Healthcare Financial Management*, V. 59, No. 2, February 2005.

Joseph Goedert, "Outsourcing: Before and After the Contract Is Signed," *Health Data Management*, March 2004, http://healthdatamanagement.com/HDMSearchResultsDetails.cfm?articleId=9568 (accessed August 19, 2006).

Michael G. McElroy, "Automation and Technology Resources for Small Medical Groups," *MGMA Connexion*, V. 5, No. 8, September 2005.

QUESTION 64

When a physician leaves a group practice, who owns the medical records?

State laws determine whether the patient records belong to the practice or the patient. Additionally, you should determine whether the physician's employment contract addresses this issue. If there isn't a law or contract amendment addressing the issue within your state, you should still plan on keeping the records. Patients who follow the departing physician can request that you send copies of their records to the physician. Obtain a signed release form that is kept with the patients' original charts. Inform the physician that you will retain the records for the time required by state law, until the malpractice statute of limitations is reached, or even beyond this length of time if requested.

You may want to update all of your physician employment agreements to ensure that the practice's rights to keep the records are specified. You could also add a noncompete clause to the agreement, depending on state regulations.

Source:

Kristie Perry, "Practice Management Q & As," *Medical Economics,* September 2004, www.memag.com/memag/article/articleDetail.jsp?id=120985&searchString =management%20system%20selection (accessed August 20, 2006).

QUESTION

We're running out of space for our medical records. How long do I need to keep records?

Medical records should be retained for the length of the statute of limitations for malpractice actions. Because the statue of limitations varies from state to state, ask your state medical board, state health department, or your practice's attorney for this information.

Inactive records on adult patients should be kept at least seven years. Keep pediatric records at least seven years past the patients' age of majority. The American Health Information Management Association (AHIMA) recommends that adult patient records be retained for 10 years beyond the most recent encounter, and pediatric records up to the age of majority plus the statute of limitations.

You should also check your physicians' malpractice coverage. How long is the coverage in force? This information may guide you in the length of time to keep medical records – well beyond the term of the coverage.

The Centers for Medicare & Medicaid Services has online information about records retention for specific documents at www.cms.gov.

Keep X-rays and other imaging records, raw psychological testing data, fetal monitoring tracings, electroencephalograms, electrocardiograms, and other records for at least five years. AHIMA advises that master patient/person indexes, birth and death registries, and registries of surgical procedures should be kept permanently.

If you are short of space for records within your facility, you may want to store inactive patients' charts in an off-site facility. Make sure that the facility is HIPAA compliant and protected from natural or human-caused disasters. You can also investigate the possibility of converting your records to an electronic health record (EHR) system.

When the retention period has passed and you destroy the records, make sure you are compliant with applicable state regulations and the HIPAA Standards for Electronic Security for disposing of medical records. Destroy paper documents by shredding them to ensure they cannot be read or recovered. Delete electronic documents and database records by wiping them from local, network, and backup drives and/or disks. Erasing information from storage media may not be sufficient because hackers may have means of accessing the information. Electronic media such as CDs, DVDs, and electronic tapes should be physically destroyed or have their data-bearing layers removed. You may want to hire a professional service to shred the paper documents and destroy the electronic media.

Sources:

Peter F. Dempsey, "Know-How: Talking Trash: Options for the Storage and Disposal of Medical Records," *MGMA Connexion*, V. 4, No. 3, March 2004.

Lisa H. Schneck, "Size Matters: To Have and to Hold – But for How Long, Guidelines for Records Retention," *MGMA Connexion*, V. 2, No. 4, April 2002.

QUESTION 66

I'm trying to decide whether to outsource transcription services. What are the costs compared to doing it in house?

Transcription services today offer a variety of options with widely varying costs. You will have to review the options and analyze the costs compared to the services and costs of your current operations. The information below provides a brief overview and analysis of the options available today.

Networking with your peers will also help you understand how other practices have dealt with this question.

Advantages to outsourcing include:

- Cost savings;
- Availability of qualified transcriptionists;
- Ability to take advantage of new dictation and transcription technology without the capital expenditure; and
- Improved physician satisfaction and operational efficiencies with benefits of new technology, including quicker turnaround.

Disadvantages of outsourcing include:

- Decreased control of the service;
- Expense (if it is less expensive to keep transcription services in house);
- Expenses related to having a quick turnaround; and
- Privacy and security concerns.

To determine your current expenses, calculate the expenses for salaries and benefits for the transcriptionists and supervisors and the supplies and equipment expenses. Include additional expenses such as cost of the space, employee taxes for the transcriptionist, cost of any outsourcing that may be used for rush requests, and costs of department turnover. Total these expenses and divide by the number of transcribed lines per year to arrive at a benchmark for comparing with contract services.

One option for medical transcription continues to be the independent transcriptionist or small company who works from physicians' handwritten notes or tapes. Charges vary, but they are usually based on a cost per line. A growing number of companies use personnel overseas, particularly India, to handle transcriptions. It is estimated that, today, only about 5 percent of transcriptions are handled overseas. Concerns over security issues related to outsourcing overseas may be delaying its expansion.

Speech or voice recognition systems have been adopted by many health care organizations. The benefits of direct capture of physician notes were once thought to be the solution to transcription worries. There continue to be issues, however, that hinder its adoption; these include:

➤ Differences in individual speech patterns;

➤ The system's ability to handle ambiguity;

➤ Interference from background noise; and

➤ The need to correct punctuation and grammar.

Currently, physicians must "train" voice recognition systems to recognize their speech patterns, and a physician or transcriptionist must review the transcripts for punctuation and grammar errors. Costs related to these delays must be factored in with the cost of purchasing the hardware and software to determine the total costs. However, the practice should still realize an overall savings in time and costs once the system is fully implemented.

After the type of service is selected, you will need to evaluate and compare vendors. Develop a list of questions, needed functions, and evaluation guidelines. You may want to develop a request for proposal (RFP) for this step. (See Question #57 for more information on RFPs.) Ask the transcriptionist or vendor the following questions:

➤ What security measures are in place to ensure data integrity and HIPAA compliance?

➤ Is their system compliant with your current electronic health record or other information system?

➤ Can their system be accessed by telephone or Internet?

- How are the charges determined? Is there a charge per line, per page, or per word? Are there any additional charges, including for rush requests?
- What is the guaranteed turnaround time?
- How is quality measured and what guarantees are provided?

Ask for a test with their system and a sample of your files. Use their list of references to ask current users about their satisfaction with the service and issues that have arisen.

Sources:

Joseph Conn, "Not Dead Yet," *Modern Healthcare*, V. 35, No. 27, July 11, 2005.

Bryan Smith, "The 'Write' Choice: A Primer on Outsourcing Transcription Services," *Healthcare Financial Management*, V. 60, No. 2, February 2006.

Nick van Terheyden, "Is Speech Recognition the Holy Grail?" *Health Management Technology*, V. 26, No. 2, February 2005.

QUESTION 67

I'd like to develop a policy regarding photocopying records when patients request copies. Can we charge for copying?

The HIPAA Privacy Rule permits health care organizations to impose reasonable photocopying fees based on cost. You should also investigate state regulations regarding copying. HIPAA regulations state that the fee may include only the cost of copying (including supplies and labor) and postage if the patient requests that the copy be mailed. If the patient has agreed to receive a summary or explanation of his or her protected health information, the covered entity may also charge a fee for preparation of the summary or explanation. The fee may not include costs associated with searching for and retrieving the requested information. (See 45 C.F.R. § 164.524.)

Source:

Medical Group Management Association, Government Affairs Department, "HHS Releases New Medical Privacy Q & As," www.mgma.com/members/advocacy/medprivacyqas.cfm (accessed August 20, 2006).

Sample Procedure for Patient Access to Medical Information

a. Upon written request, and with reasonable notice, the Practice provides a patient or designee with a copy of the medical record.
    1) If the patient chooses, copies of the "pertinent" portion of the record may be obtained.
    2) The Practice responds in 30 days unless the record is off the premises.
    3) If it is off the premises, then the Practice responds in 60 days.
    4) If extenuating circumstances arise, the Practice provides written notice that it needs an extension for an additional 30 days.
b. The Practice releases the entire medical record as authorized by the patient, including notes and information contained from an outside provider.
c. Requests for medical records must contain:
    1) The name and address of the patient and provider;
    2) The person or organization to which information is to be released;
    3) A statement that the request may be revoked by the patient;
    4) The specific information requested;
    5) The date of the request;
    6) The purpose and the signature of the patient; and
    7) A statement that the request complies with these regulations, and has been approved by the attorney.
d. If a patient requests a copy of health information, the Practice may charge a reasonable, cost-based fee for the copying. (See related policy 5.17 on Medical Record Duplication and Form Completion in the *Operating Policies & Procedures Manual for Medical Practices*.)

Source: Elizabeth W. Woodcock, MBA, FACMPE, CPC, and Bette A. Warne, CMPE, *Operating Policies & Procedures Manual for Medical Practices,* 3rd Edition (Englewood, CO: Medical Group Management Association, 2006).

QUESTION 68

Can medical records be included in a practice valuation? How is their value determined?

Practice valuations do not typically include the value per se of the medical records. There is no guarantee that the patients will remain with the practice after it is sold, and state law may specify that the records are owned by the patients rather than the practice. The number of patients (with active charts) may be considered as part of the goodwill value or in determining the income of the practice.

Some valuations calculate the number of records that will be transferred to the buyer and determine the charges/payments from those patients over the previous two years in order to determine the potential income they represented. Others use the net income (total revenue minus operating expenses) for the value of all of the medical records.

Occasionally, there is a reason to place a specific value on medical records. Various consultants have placed values from $10 to $60 based on the market and specialty of the practice.

To ensure you receive an accurate valuation, you should probably hire a practice valuation expert or medical practice consultant. Also, remember that patients must be contacted prior to their record being transferred to another physician.

Sources:

"Party Line: Buying Charts," *MGMA Connexion*, V. 4, No. 8, September 2004.

Kristie Perry, "Practice Management Q & A," *Medical Economics*, April 10, 2000, www.memag.com/memag/article/articleDetail.jsp?id=124110&searchString=chart%20value (accessed August 20, 2006).

CHAPTER 6
Planning and Marketing

QUESTION 69

I need some help in conducting market research. How do I find out what our market share is?

Medical practices have a variety of reasons to conduct market research. They want to determine their market share, measure patient satisfaction, decide whether a new service should be offered, and find information to support their strategic planning. Market research can be a complex process to ensure that accurate information is gathered, so you may want to hire a marketing specialist to conduct the research.

While market share may be an interesting metric for your practice, be sure that you don't get caught up in that one statistic. It is important to track various trends so that you understand whether or not your practice is growing, and so that you can compare that information to that of the market. The rest of this section will discuss this in greater detail, along with market research in general.

You will first need to determine the objective of the market research. What questions do you have? What information is needed? How will the results aid in your decision making? Determining the goals of the research will result in the right information being gathered. The more targeted the research, the more usable the results will be.

Once the goals are determined, how important is the information to the practice and the decision making? This will help determine how much time and effort to expend. If it is "nice to have" information, you may do a quick survey or use information already available in the literature or from some other secondary source. If it is vital information or a substantial amount of money rests on making the correct

A CLOSER LOOK...

Market Share Analysis

To determine if your practice is maintaining its market share for specific services, use a combination of internal and external research. Gather external data on the number of procedures that are performed in a year and the past several years along with general demographics information. Obtain the data from community hospitals, private firms, or the National Center for Healthcare Statistics (www.cdc.gov/nchs). The amount of detail available will depend on your location, the services you are analyzing, and how much you are willing to pay for the data. You should look at data specific to your community if at all possible.

Pull together information from your practice on the number of procedures and your patient demographics. Look at the typical number of procedures per population and how that number has changed over several years. What is the size of your community, and how many of these procedures did your practice perform last year and in the preceding years? How do your patients compare with the population in the external data? How did the trend data compare to your trend data?

If the number of procedures in your practice has not kept pace with the trend in the general population, then you may be losing market share. You may want to increase your marketing efforts or add another physician.

Source: Michael C. Boblitz, "Know-How: Knowledge is Advantage: Using Market Research for Competitive Intelligence," *MGMA Connexion*, V. 6, No. 1, January 2006.

---

decision, a thorough research project is necessary. You may want to conduct a return-on-investment (ROI) analysis to calculate the value of the project compared to the costs of the research.

The market research methodology can be selected after the goals and ROI are determined:

- **Internal vs. external research** – You may already have the data you need from your own information systems, employees, previous studies, and board members. Research can be conducted using professional associations, published literature, and Internet resources.

- **Quantitative vs. qualitative research** – Are specific numbers, statistics, or percentages needed, or are opinions, anecdotes, or feelings more appropriate?

- **Market segments** – Divide your total audience into specific targets such as gender, age, race, economic status, and geographic location. Information is then used to develop products or marketing methods to reach the specific segments.

- **Value analysis or positioning research** – How do your customers value your organization and its services, and how does it compare with the competition or other services?

There are several options for gathering quantitative or qualitative information from a population:

- **Telephone, mail, and Web-based surveys** provide quantitative results, can be used to track trends, and reach a larger percentage of a targeted group. They are limited to multiple-choice, ranking, and short answers. They are also less in-depth and flexible than other options.

- **Focus groups** gather in-depth, qualitative information and are more flexible than surveys, enabling the facilitator to gather even more detailed information. The results aren't quantitative and assume that the group members are representative of the total market.

- **One-on-one interviews** collect opinions and feelings about the questions in more depth than with a focus group.

➤ **Secret shoppers** are used to investigate business operations and customer service from the customer's perspective.

Which option you choose will depend on your goals, which should vary from one project to the next. You may even use a combination of options, starting with a Web-based survey and then using focus groups or interviews to pinpoint answers to questions raised by the survey.

Source:

Daniel Fell, "Practical Market Research for Healthcare Marketers," *COR Healthcare Market Strategist*, V. 2, No. 4, April 2001.

QUESTION 70

We are considering a merger of several internal medicine groups in hopes of gaining efficiency from economies of scale. Can you provide information on the advantages and disadvantages of these types of mergers?

Many physicians see mergers as a means of growing their practice and sharing operating expenses. It is difficult, however, to combine separate organizations and cultures into one. Therefore, a thorough analysis of the reasons for the merger and the vision for the final organization need to occur.

Economies of scale may indeed be obtained if the merger is complete and the separate practices become one with a united culture and fully shared operations. There will not be a reduction of operating cost if each practice continues to operate in its premerger fashion. The merger must take place with a common vision of the merged practice, not just with the dollar signs of expected increased compensation. (See Question #78 for more information on economies of scale and group practice size.)

Mergers should follow these four basic steps:

> *"The mergers that work take longer than the ones that don't work. The message is this: Hasty mergers are likely not to go very far. Those that are thought out – How are we going to operate? What will our value system and practice philosophy be? – are the ones that work."*
>
> —William Jessee, MD, FACMPE, President and CEO of MGMA, in: Michael Romano, "More Docs Say: Super-size it," *Modern Healthcare*, V. 34, No. 40, October 4, 2004, pp. 24-35.

1. **Strategy** – Why is the merger wanted? What are the goals? Does it make sense?

2. **Due diligence** – What are the differences among the participants and what are the solutions? How do the cultures differ? How do the vision and values statements differ? The analysis must include asset valuation, leadership structure, administrative selection, compensation plan, and benefits. Once the analysis is complete, a business plan including benchmarks, timetable, and accountabilities should be developed.

3. **Execution** – Merge all the components together into one, including patient services, information systems, and human resources. Develop a new name, fee schedule, organizational documents, and marketing materials.

4. **Making it work** – The cultures blend to become one organization. This may be the lengthiest aspect of the merger. Ideas to encourage the blending include retreats, staff meetings, and strong, supportive leadership.

There is no guarantee that any merger will succeed, but having the right goals for the merger and following these four

A CLOSER LOOK...

Common reasons for mergers include:

✔ Increased clout for negotiating with health plans;

✔ Shared resources for handling the complexities of medical practice management and regulatory compliance;

✔ Enhanced ability to add ancillary services;

✔ Greater community recognition; and

✔ Professional camaraderie.

---

steps will increase the odds and can result in an improved organization for the benefit of all.

Sources:

Robert C. Bohlmann, "Insights: Bigger Again ... But Better?" *MGMA Connexion*, V. 3, No. 1, January 2003.

Robert C. Bohlmann, "Mergers and Affiliation," *Directions Newsletter*, V. 5, No. 3, 2003.

Roberta N. Clarke, DBA, "Medical Practice Marketing Management," in *Physician Practice Management: Essential Operational and Financial Knowledge*, ed. Lawrence F. Wolper, MBA, FACMPE (Sudbury, MA: Jones and Bartlett Publishers, 2005), pp. 175–176.

QUESTION 71

We're developing our strategic plan and would like to determine the number and specialty of physicians who should serve a community of our size. How do I access data of this type?

You should follow these five steps to determine the physician need for your community:

1. Define the geographic region that you serve. Depending on the community and your goals, you may want to include areas beyond your immediate neighborhood or community. You may need to obtain data from hospitals or local health organizations to

identify the geographic perimeters of the population that seeks health services within your community.

2. Calculate the population within the medical service area using the local chamber of commerce data or U.S. Census Bureau (www.census.gov).

3. Identify the providers and specialties within the area using information from local business directories or the state medical board.

4. Apply calculations from physician-to-population ratio studies.

5. Gather information from your local hospitals regarding their physician staff development plans.

There were several studies in the 1980s and 1990s to determine the ideal ratio of physicians and specialties per population. However, they varied widely depending on the market characteristics (high managed care or not) and the ideas of the authors. Because of their age, these studies may not reflect current health care demand and services. Therefore, they should be used with caution.

The following is a brief summary of the most frequently cited studies:

➤ **Graduate Medical Education National Advisory Committee (GMENAC)** – Published in 1980, this government-sponsored study remains the most widely cited. Its physician-to-population ratio of one physician to 522 people tends to be higher than studies that take into account managed care. It concluded that primary care physicians should make up 36 percent of the physician pool and that specialists should handle 64 percent of cases.

➤ **Hicks-Glenn** – In this 1989 study, physician needs were calculated by multiplying the average annual physician encounters (the population using a specialty) by the population to be served and dividing that

> **KEY POINT**
>
> *Paying attention to forecasts is important, but determining what's best for your practice is too complicated to let one study or report influence you too heavily. Those statistics are only one factor in the decision to hire.*

number by the annual number of patient encounters that the specialty generally handles (as determined by benchmarking data).

- **Weiner** – This 1994 study compares traditional health care to a managed care environment. It provides adjusted ratios that take into account managed care population statistics such as age, gender, and Medicaid or uninsured status; patients who choose out-of-network services; and physician productivity. This study determined the lowest physician-to-population ratio of all the studies: one primary care physician per 1,538 people, and up to 30 percent fewer specialists than other models recommend.

The Health Policy Institute of the Medical College of Wisconsin at Milwaukee predicts that in 2010, the nation will be 50,000 physicians short of the number needed. It also foresees that by 2015, nearly 500,000 nonphysician providers will assist 25 percent of the physician work force. According to its 2000 study, current shortages exist in general surgery and many subspecialties, whereas there is a glut of primary care physicians.

Richard D. Hansen, MGMA Health Care Consulting Group, says that paying attention to forecasts is important, but determining what's best for your practice is too complicated to let one study or report influence you too heavily. "If you hear about an expected population growth or an increase in birth rates in your area, take that into account, but remember that those statistics are only one factor in the decision to hire," he says.

Physician-to-population ratios are frequently used to develop a physician-needs assessment or plan for growth opportunities or other changes. Because of the debate over the studies, you should also look at additional data including:

➤ Changes in demands among your patients to identify what services they are looking for and what services are less in demand;

➤ Changes in demographics of your community to help in identifying how demands may change for health care services in the future;

➤ Information from hospitals and health plans showing their recommendations for the populations they are serving; and

➤ Analysis of the competition to identify their strengths that you may not want to compete against and their weaknesses that might provide you with a competitive edge.

Sources:

Ariana Harner, "Size Matters: Counting Heads. Determine Appropriate Physician-to-Population Ratios for Your Practice," *MGMA Connexion*, V. 2, No. 9, October 2002.

Todd Grages, "Developing a Physician Needs Assessment," *MGM Journal*, V. 48, No. 3, May/June 2001.

Daniel P. Stech, MBA, "Physician-to-Population Ratios: What Are We Really Talking About?" in *Performance and Practices of Successful Medical Groups: 2003 Report Based on 2002 Data* (Englewood, CO: Medical Group Management Association, 2003), pp. 24-27.

QUESTION 72

What do I need to know to conduct a successful patient loyalty survey in our practice?

Patients who have not developed a sense of loyalty to your practice will become inactive patients, and they will not recommend your practice to others. It is important to conduct loyalty surveys on a regular basis and in a manner that paints an accurate picture of patients' perceptions of your practice. In a sense, satisfied patients mean nothing, and loyal patients mean everything.

The most important factor in a successful survey is asking the right questions in the best format. Identify the goal of the survey and develop questions to achieve the goal. If you want to gauge overall loyalty, the questions will address more issues than if a specific topic needs to be addressed. Because of the art of writing effective questions, it may be beneficial to use standardized questionnaires or enlist the aid of an experienced survey writer.

Questions that ask for a ranking (1 to 5 or poor to excellent) will provide more information than yes/no questions. Always provide room for comments so patients can explain poor ratings. Questions that are unfocused or beyond the practice's control will be wasteful; make sure every question counts. Include one or two open-ended questions to allow respondents to comment on issues not addressed in the questionnaire. Ask, for example, Is there anything else we should know about? What can we do to improve your experience with our practice?

Surveys are typically conducted anonymously. However, include an opportunity for respondents to provide contact information if there is an issue that they would like to have addressed. This does require regular monitoring of returned questionnaires and quick follow-up.

The survey should be short, with succinct questions to encourage completion. General satisfaction surveys should ask questions in the following areas:

> **Appointments and registration** – Ask about timeliness of appointments, waiting time upon arrival and in the exam room, and the check-in process.

- **Relations with staff** – Address several types of employees (receptionists, billing personnel, and so on).

- **Communication** – Include telephone service, returning messages, promptness of delivering test results, and after-hours issues.

- **Relation with physician** – Ask whether the doctor listens, spends an adequate amount of time with them, and sufficiently explains the diagnosis and treatment.

- **Facility issues** – Ask about adequate parking, difficulties in finding the practice or the specific department within the building, the comfort of the waiting room and exam room, and the hours of operation.

There are several methods for conducting surveys, each with its advantages and disadvantages. These methods include:

- Distributing questionnaires as patients check out;

- Mailing questionnaires;

- E-mailing or distributing Web-based questionnaires; and

- Calling patients by telephone.

Many practices prefer to mail the survey because it is less expensive and reaches a broader audience than telephone or e-mail. Mailed surveys have less chance of manipulation by staff or others. These survey forms should include stamped, self-addressed envelopes or be created on postage-paid postcards.

The final step to a successful survey is using the results. Review the responses to identify areas that need to be addressed. Don't assume that "good" ratings don't need to be

A CLOSER LOOK...

Better Performing Group Case Study

Montana Heart Institute, Billings, Mont., hands out patient satisfaction surveys at the end of each visit. Practice manager Dianne Schleuning, MPH, NHA, reviews each completed survey, including the open-ended questions. "The comments in the open-ended questions reveal much more of what the patient really thinks about the practice and the care provided," says Schleuning.

The practice's emphasis on quality care and patient satisfaction is reflected in the high scores on the satisfaction surveys. When a negative comment is received, staff members develop a plan to address the issue.

Source: "Success Story: Montana Heart Institute," in *Performance and Practices of Successful Medical Groups: 2005 Report Based on 2004 Data* (Englewood, CO: Medical Group Management Association, 2005), pp. 213-216.

---

addressed. Respondents may be hesitant to rate the practice too poorly even when something does bother them. You may need to use a telephone survey or other method to pinpoint specific causes of dissatisfaction. For example, you may not know if a poor rating about telephone communication is due to being on hold too long or difficulty in navigating a complicated automated system.

Physicians and staff should discuss ways to improve the ratings before the next survey. Inform patients about the changes that have been made so that they know you are listening to them.

Sources:

"Improving Patient Satisfaction Can Be Data-Driven Process," *Data Strategies & Benchmarks*, V. 6, No. 10, October 2002.

Gil Weber, "Effective Patient and Referring Provider Satisfaction Surveys," *Administrative Eyecare*, V. 12, No. 2, Spring 2003.

QUESTION 73

The board has reviewed my budget and wants to reduce the marketing and advertising dollars. How can I determine what is an appropriate or typical advertising budget for medical groups?

The appropriate marketing budget for your practice will depend on your situation. Remember, though, that there is a difference between marketing and advertising – advertising is just one of many tactics used under an overall marketing plan. If your practice is new and still in the growing stage, more money will be needed for advertising and to develop and distribute promotional materials. You may need to develop two sets of materials: one devoted to potential referring physicians and another for patients.

If your practice is generating enough revenue to keep your physicians satisfied, then your marketing budget may also stabilize. Even mature, successful practices need to continue marketing to attract enough new patients to replace the patients who depart from your practice through normal turnover. Promotional materials should be used to keep in touch with current patients and referring physicians to ensure their continued satisfaction and business.

If your physicians want to increase the number of patients, develop new services, or take on an additional physician, a marketing plan and budget should reflect the dollars needed for doing these things and promoting them.

If the board is concerned about high operating costs and declining revenue, it is time to convince them of the importance of marketing to increase the practice's revenue. You should also discuss low-cost ideas for promoting the practice, such as writing articles for the local newspaper, participating in community health fairs, making the Website more functional, and meeting with referring physicians.

Source:

Christina Moschella, "Know-How: Step Right Up! Marketing Your Medical Practice," *MGMA Connexion*, V. 4, No. 2, February 2004.

A CLOSER LOOK...

Medical Practice Advertising Costs

To benchmark your marketing budget with other medical practices, look at data in the MGMA *Cost Survey Report*. The table below shows the percentage of total medical revenue that practices spend on promotion and marketing. These costs include patient newsletters, information booklets, promotional fliers, brochures, yellow page listings, and marketing or public relations consultants.

Practice type	Median percent of total medical revenue
Multispecialty	0.34%
Anesthesiology	0.05%
Family practice	0.36%
Obstetrics/Gynecology	0.62%
Orthopedic surgery	0.53%

Sources:

Medical Group Management Association, *Cost Survey for Multispecialty Practices: 2005 Report Based on 2004 Data* (Englewood, CO: Medical Group Management Association, 2005).

Medical Group Management Association, *Cost Survey for Single Specialty Practices: 2005 Report Based on 2004 Data* (Englewood, CO: Medical Group Management Association, 2005).

QUESTION 74

I've heard about urgent care centers or "minute clinics." Can you tell me more about these facilities and how to develop one?

Urgent care centers, or "emergicenters," have been around for many years. A new twist on these facilities is the "minute clinic" or "quick care center." Both types of facilities are options for medical practices looking for ways to generate more revenue or increase their presence in the market.

These walk-in centers do not require scheduled appointments or established relationships with the providers. They typically provide extended hours during weekday evenings and on some weekends. Fees are less than those in the hospital emergency rooms, but they may be more than a family physician's charges. Patients that require continued treatment may be referred to a physician in the main practice.

The National Association for Ambulatory Urgent Care (NAFAC) defines urgent care as facilities that treat episodic and acute medical problems fully corrected in seven to fourteen days. "The services are typically provided seven days each week, on average 13 hours each day, and an appointment is not required. Physician and medical staffs are full time providers in the UCC [urgent care center] clinic." Urgent care centers treat "minor lacerations, fractures, sore throats, ear infections, upper respiratory infections, and other 'just don't feel good' conditions."

Urgent care centers are staffed with at least one physician, typically board certified in family practice or emergency medicine. Physicians may be compensated on an hourly basis or based on productivity or another measure to ensure commitment to the facility's success. UCC facilities may include procedure rooms for lacerations and fractures, a radiology department, and a laboratory. They are fully staffed to support their physicians and additional services.

Patients may use urgent care centers because they don't have insurance coverage, so most centers collect payment at the time of service. New centers may require extensive

> **KEY POINT**
>
> *New urgent care centers may require extensive promotion to build the awareness and patient base to make them self-sustaining, especially with the difficulty of collecting payment from patients.*

A CLOSER LOOK...

Quick Care kiosks in Milwaukee

Aurora Health Care system in Milwaukee set up two Aurora Quick Care kiosks in their pharmacies for $80,000. Patients pay $30 for most services vs. $133 or more at Aurora's emergency department. The nurse practitioners can do seven common tests and assess the patients' symptoms. Visits typically take 10 to 15 minutes. Patients are referred to primary care physicians or emergency rooms for more serious conditions.

---

promotion to build the awareness and patient base to make them self-sustaining, especially with the difficulty of collecting payment from patients.

Other keys to running a successful urgent care center are the same as for nonurgent care practices. These include:

- ➤ Maximizing patient flow;
- ➤ Ensuring accurate coding and claims submission;
- ➤ Emphasizing patient satisfaction;
- ➤ Using quality staff; and
- ➤ Monitoring the financial picture.

Minute clinics, or quick clinics, are newer developments. These facilities are typically located within a retail store, grocery store, or pharmacy. Physician extenders rather than physicians staff the clinics. They serve patients who have minor ailments or concerns and are looking for convenience without waiting for appointments. Minute clinics are more limited than urgent care centers in their services, handling only a limited set of medical problems. Payment may be by "cash only" for charges less than $40. Some clinics have been forced to accept Medicare and other insurance coverage to maintain their visit numbers.

Your practice should know where these clinics are and who staffs them. You may wish to consider developing relationships with the providers, so that in the case of a referral, your practice will be high on the list.

Sources:

Robert Kazel, "Demand for Convenience Puts Clinics in Stores," *American Medical News*, September 13, 2004, www.ama-assn.org/amednews/2004/09/13/bil20913.htm (accessed October 12, 2004).

Mike Norbut, "Urgent Need for Extra Revenue? Some Try Urgent Care," *American Medical News*, V. 46, No. 16, April 28, 2003.

Diana Revell, "Lessons to Be Learned From Urgent Care Centers," ACMPE Professional Paper (Englewood, CO: American College of Medical Practice Executives, 2002), www3.mgma.com/articles/index.cfm?fuseaction=detail.main&articleID=12311 (accessed August 27, 2006).

Julie Sneider, "Just the Basics: Aurora Launching Quick Care Sites in Pharmacies, Stores," *The Business Journal of Milwaukee*, March 26, 2004, www.bizjournals.com/industries/health_care/physician_practices/2004/03/29/milwaukee_stories (accessed March 29, 2004).

National Association for Ambulatory Urgent Care, "About NAFAC," www.urgentcare.org/AboutNAFAC (accessed August 27, 2006).

QUESTION 75

How do I get started on writing a strategic plan for our medical group?

The strategic plan assesses marketplace trends, goals for the organization's future, and fulfillment of the mission and vision. To be effective, the planning process must include the key stakeholders. Small practices should include all of its physicians in the strategic planning process. Larger groups may wish to limit participation to 10 or 12 physicians and elicit feedback and analysis from others through surveys, interviews, and updates.

You should conduct a strategic planning retreat to allow participants to focus on the task at hand. During the retreat, participants will identify current issues and challenges, examine internal and external influences (an analysis of strengths, weaknesses, opportunities, and threats, or SWOT

A CLOSER LOOK...

Questions to ask while gathering information before planning a retreat

- ✔ What are your expectations for this strategic planning retreat?
- ✔ How would you describe this practice?
- ✔ What are the top three issues facing the practice?
- ✔ What do you want the practice to look like in the next one to three years?
- ✔ Do you have any other comments?

Source: Richard D. Hansen, "Strategic Planning: Your Road Map to Success," *MGMA Directions,* V. 4, No. 1, Winter 2002.

---

analysis), discuss the organization's mission and vision, and set a limited number of goals for the next one to three years. The retreat should be held off-site to minimize disruptions, and it should be run by a facilitator, preferably someone from outside of the organization.

To ensure effective planning retreats, analysis materials should be prepared in advance. These may include a competitive analysis, information on health care and demographic trends, and a SWOT analysis of the practice. Information can be gathered using an informal survey or interviews with the physicians and employees. The survey may also include questions about the vision and the perceived goals of the strategic planning process. These materials will serve as a starting point during the retreat. (See "A Closer Look" for sample questions.)

Participants in the retreat should identify organizational goals for the next three to five years. The goals should be realistic and aligned with the group's mission and vision.

The strategic plan itself will include:

- ➤ A competitive analysis;

- ➤ External factors such as demographic trends and regulatory challenges;

- ➤ An analysis of your strengths, weaknesses, opportunities, staffing, service capacity, and financial health;

- ➤ An examination of the career needs of physicians and their succession, if appropriate;

- ➤ The needs of the group; and

- ➤ The strategic goals identified during the retreat and planning process.

Share the strategic plan and goals with the rest of the organization in all-staff or departmental meetings. Express the commitment to the strategic plan and how the goals will be accomplished. Identify at a departmental or organization-wide level the tactics required to achieve the goals and the means of measuring success.

The strategic plan will not be effective if it is filed away. Your organization must be committed to the plan and apply the tactics to reach the goals. All the physicians and employees must understand their roles and be committed to the plan's success.

FOR MORE INFORMATION . . .

The following strategic planning tools are available on the MGMA Website, www.mgma.com/members/tools/index.cfm:

- ✔ Environmental assessment planning tool;
- ✔ PEST (political, economic, social, and technological) force analysis tool; and
- ✔ SWOT (strength, weaknesses, opportunities, and threats) analysis tool.

Sources:

Hobart Collins, "Quick Tip: Formal Strategic Planning Demands Commitment," *MGMA e-Connexion,* Issue 66, November 2004.

Andrea DeRosier, "Size Matters: Goal-Oriented: A Strategic Planning Case Study," *MGMA Connexion,* V. 5, No. 6, July 2005.

Richard D. Hansen, "Strategic Planning: It's Worth the Effort: Homework Makes Retreats Work," *MGMA Connexion,* V. 3, No. 8, September 2003.

QUESTION 76

I'm looking for additional revenue for the practice. How can I determine which ancillary or other services are the best match for our group?

Many medical practices seek new revenue opportunities from ancillary services. As reimbursement declines and operating costs escalate, adding services to generate profit has great appeal. But success in diversification will only come with the right strategy, physician buy-in, and a carefully planned approach.

You and the practice leaders should examine your options honestly and hold planning meetings that emphasize open discussion. Begin by composing a list of potential opportunities. Ask the physicians and other key stakeholders, "What types of services that are consistent with our core business activities and service lines could we deliver that we're not delivering today?" Look to your market and its needs in defining potential services.

Ancillary opportunities include diagnostic services, in-office and independent clinical laboratories, investments in ambulatory surgery centers, new treatments, procedures and products consistent with the group's specialty (such as bariatric surgery, cosmetic services, and vein clinics), and alternative and complementary treatments.

Primary care practices may offer MRI, CT, echocardiography, bone densitometry, and other imaging services that build on the purpose of their missions. Specialty practices

> **KEY POINT**
>
>  As reimbursement declines and operating costs escalate, adding services to generate profit has great appeal. But success in diversification will only come with the right strategy, physician buy-in, and a carefully planned approach.

add to their core mix of clinical and surgical services. For example, cardiology practices could offer a variety of diagnostic and other services previously found only in hospitals, such as electrocardiograms, stress tests, nuclear medicine, and, in some communities, in-office catheterization. Multispecialty practices should evaluate which services are currently referred out that could be provided in-house.

Discuss these options. Does your practice have the resources and expertise to implement them? Do they fit in with the obligations of a medical business – providing clinically appropriate services from competent providers in a legally compliant manner? Evaluate whether your organization has advantages in clinical expertise, management, or market position. Determine whether any of these factors will limit the success of the strategy.

In determining the feasibility of each revenue alternative, consider external factors potentially affecting the implementation and success, including:

➤ Third-party reimbursement trends;

➤ Demographics of your market;

➤ Service-area economic conditions and stability;

➤ Federal and state regulations and opportunities; and

➤ Current and potential competition.

Also weigh internal factors within your control, such as:

➤ Current quality of care and patient services;

➤ Operational conditions and efficiency;

➤ Access to and willingness to devote capital to the venture; and

➤ Management expertise.

Use the strategic planning process (see Question #75) to clarify the practice's mission and goals, and conduct a SWOT analysis. Conduct a planning retreat for open discussion of the opportunity, including issues and concerns. The retreat should clarify the goals of the proposed new services and the plan for implementation.

The federal and state regulations that must be considered include the Stark law, antikickback regulations, federal reimbursement laws, state certification-of-need requirements, and state licensure issues. Phase I final rule of the Stark law (January 4, 2002) listed ancillary service exemptions for medical practices, including the "in-office ancillary service exemption" and nuclear medicine procedures, ambulatory surgery centers, and certain diagnostic services.

Antikickback regulations will come into effect with joint ventures and contractual and service relationships involving two or more medical groups, hospitals, or other health care providers. A thorough review of these regulations and their exemptions should be included as part of the planning process.

Sources:

Bruce A. Johnson and Gerald A. Niederman, "Expanding Beyond Professional Service Revenue: Experiences, Regulatory Issues and Lessons Learned," *APA Matrix*, V. 18, No. 2, April 2005.

Bruce A. Johnson, Darrell L. Schryver, and Daniel P. Stech, *Building Practice Revenue: A Guide to Developing New Services* (Englewood, CO: Medical Group Management Association, 2003).

QUESTION 77

How do I increase the number of referrals we receive from primary care physicians?

Prior to referring to your practice, primary care physicians need to know about your physicians, their specialties, and what makes your practice unique. They are more apt to refer patients to physicians with whom they have developed a relationship. Flashy promotional brochures and gifts are not as effective as name recognition.

You can use options already in place to increase your physicians' visibility in the community. Physicians should be encouraged to attend hospital-sponsored events and rounds. They should participate in hospital committees and lecture programs or write articles for hospital newsletters. Local medical societies' meetings and newsletters are a great way to meet more physicians and increase awareness.

Your practice may want to sponsor an open house or an educational series to demonstrate how your practice is unique. You might hand out small items, like a referral note pad or information items, to keep your name in front of the physicians.

After you've created awareness, you need to secure the referring relationship. The physicians, an administrator, or a referral manager should be available to welcome new referrers and build the relationship. Share information on your practice's hours, your physicians' expertise, the insurance plans you accept, and so on. Learn as much as possible about the referring physicians and their practice.

Referring physicians will have several expectations of your practice, which your practice should meet or exceed; these include:

> **KEY POINT**
>
>  Primary care physicians need to know about your physicians, their specialties, and what makes your practice unique. They are more apt to refer patients to physicians with whom they have developed a relationship. Flashy promotional brochures and gifts are not as effective as name recognition.

➤ An easy process for setting up appointments, which includes having a direct telephone number or a dedicated extension for referrals, and a process for returning telephone calls as soon as possible;

➤ A reasonable time frame for available appointments;

➤ Frequent communication about the patients' status, with initial calls and follow-ups made on a regular basis;

➤ A professional and friendly staff; and

➤ Respect for the referring physician and an appreciation of the referrals.

To ensure a continuing relationship, conduct annual referring-physician satisfaction surveys. Include questions about communication, ease in setting up appointments, quality of care, and the relationship with staff. The survey will help in identifying problems that need to be corrected.

Sources:

Mike Norbut, "You Schmooze, You Lose: How to Win Referrals and Influence Doctors," *American Medical News*, V. 46, No. 5, February 3, 2003, www.ama-assn.org/sci-pubs/amnews/pick_03/bisa0203.htm (accessed February 13, 2003).

"Reach Out to Referrals and Increase Patient Base," *The Doctor's Office*, Issue 266, July 2004.

Gil Weber, "Effective Patient and Referring Provider Satisfaction Surveys," *Administrative Eyecare*, V. 12, No. 2, Spring 2003.

QUESTION 78

We're trying to decide if we should add more physicians to our practice. What is the ideal size of a group practice in terms of number of physicians? How many physicians enable the practice to operate at maximum productivity and efficiencies of scale?

Several factors make it difficult to determine the ideal number of physicians in a group practice. Maximum productivity and efficiencies of scale are only part of the picture. Additional factors include managed care market penetration, the group type (whether single or multispecialty), and your physicians' preferences.

The 1990s were a time of increasing managed care and increasing administrative costs. Operating costs for group practices rose from 44.3 percent in 1965 to 63.3 percent in 2004, according to data from MGMA's *Cost Survey Report*. Solo practices and small groups found it difficult to compete and deal with the changes.

Merging into larger, multispecialty groups seemed to be a solution. The larger number of physicians could share in the operating costs. Including primary care physicians made the practice more attractive to managed care plans, and they provided a source of referrals for the specialists. A 2002 study on the economies of scale of multispecialty practices found that groups of 26 to 50 physicians had the best financial picture when comparing total operating costs, physician compensation, accounts receivable, and revenue.

The additional benefits of large, multispecialty groups include:

➤ The ability to purchase electronic health record and practice management systems;

➤ Expanded quality of care functions;

A CLOSER LOOK...

Median number of FTE physicians in single-specialty groups

Primary care specialties (including OB/GYN)	5.6
Cardiology	11.5
Hematology/oncology	5.0
Gastroenterology	8.6
Neurology	6.5
Radiology	17.0
Anesthesiology	17.9
General surgery	6.3
Orthopedic surgery	14.0
Otorhinolaryngology	5.0
Urology	5.3

Note: FTE = full-time-equivalent

Source: Medical Group Management Association, *Cost Survey for Single-Specialty Practices: 2005 Report Based on 2004 Data* (Englewood, CO: Medical Group Management Association, 2005).

➤ Patient convenience; and

➤ Physician interaction with colleagues.

There is still an interest in large multispecialty practices, with some growing to 200 and even 700 physicians. However, because the strength of managed care has changed since the 1990s, physicians are moving back to smaller or single-specialty practices. The percentage of group practices with more than 20 physicians declined from 71.6 percent in 1998 to 43.2 percent in 2000–2001.

Many specialists have found advantages in forming large single-specialty groups. They are freed from subsidizing primary care physicians, which typically occurs in multispecialty practices. Compensation levels are typically highest in single-specialty groups.

Additional benefits of larger single-specialty groups include:

➤ The ability to invest in information systems and ancillary services;

➤ Managed care negotiation strength;

➤ Increased visibility in the community;

➤ Improved ability to provide quality care; and

➤ Better administrative expertise for handling business and regulatory complexity.

The majority of physicians continue to practice in smaller practices. In 2004, about 69 percent of MGMA member practices were groups with 10 or fewer physicians. Primary care physicians are more likely to be in smaller groups. The ideal size may be five to 10 physicians. Practices with more than 10 physicians see an increase in operating expenses and a more complex organizational structure than they may desire. Practices with one to three physicians may not have enough revenue to handle the costs of management and regulatory complexity.

Judging from the available data and practice trends, the ideal size of your group practice will depend on the influence of managed care in your market, decisions on how you want to approach health plans, and whether you are a single- or multispecialty practice and primary care or specialty. The final factor will be which type of practice your physicians prefer.

Sources:

Thomas P. Weil, "Multispecialty Physician Practices: Fixed and Variable Costs, and Economies of Scale," *Journal of Ambulatory Care Management*, V. 25, No. 3, July 2002.

Michael Romano, "More Docs Say: Super-Size It," *Modern Healthcare*, V. 34, No. 40, October 4, 2004.

Lawrence P. Casalino, "Growth of Single-Specialty Medical Groups," *Health Affairs*, V. 23, No. 2, March/April 2004.

"Practice Trends: Are Physicians Returning to Smaller Practice?" *Health Affairs*, V. 22, No. 1, January/February 2003.

QUESTION 79

A management services organization (MSO) has approached us, and I don't know if we should contract with them. What are the benefits and disadvantages of contracting with an MSO?

Management services organizations (MSOs), more common in the 1990s, were often developed by hospital and health systems as a means of affiliating more closely with physician practices. Practices contracted with the MSOs to provide various business functions, and the hospitals expected to see a return in increased ancillary services and hospital admissions.

The MSO model struggled in the past, but today it is making a comeback, having learned from previous mistakes. MSOs may still be affiliated with a health system, but they are often independent or physician-owned organizations. They are encouraging physicians to participate in the decision-making process. Also, it is important to note that physicians are now being compensated based on their productivity rather than having a set salary.

MSOs typically are contracted to provide the following administrative services:

➤ Billing and collections;

➤ Financial services;

➤ Group purchasing;

➤ Human resources management;

➤ Information systems support;

➤ Managed care contracting;

➤ Practice development support; and

➤ Provider credentialing.

Large health systems, including academic medical systems, may still use MSOs to provide centralized services and unite dispersed facilities. However, contracting with an MSO is probably more beneficial to solo and small-group practices. It is a way of sharing overhead expenses while maintaining the autonomy of a small practice. Physicians in small practices may spend too much time managing the business side themselves or employ an office manager who may not have the expertise for strategic business management. MSOs provide the experienced management, and some may offer on-site practice administrators.

Before you contract with an MSO, you should conduct the same analysis as outsourcing any function. There are advantages and disadvantages.

Advantages include:

➤ It provides potential cost savings;

➤ It provides professional expertise; and

➤ It enables physicians to concentrate on clinical services rather than business management.

Disadvantages include:

➤ It may not be cost effective;

➤ There is some loss of management control; and

➤ It can delay responses in identifying and solving problems.

If you decide that contracting with an MSO is right for your practice, investigate the following factors before signing the contract:

➤ **The financial status of the MSO.** Does it have the resources to provide what it promises? Will it be around for the length of your contract?

- **The experience of the MSO and its staff.** Do they provide the expertise in medical practice management that you are looking for? Are they experienced with your specialty?

- **The costs of their services compared with your current operating costs.** If the MSO costs are higher, are the benefits worth it? Will it free time to increase revenue? Is reducing the concerns of managing the business worth the cost?

- **The services the MSO will provide vs. those for which the practice will be responsible.** Are the responsible parties clearly defined and included in the contract?

- **The financial and operating benchmarks that the MSO must meet or exceed.** Are these benchmarks realistic? If the benchmarks are not reached, what are the consequences?

- **The terms of the contract.** Make sure you can terminate the contract within a 30- or 90-day period in case you are dissatisfied.

Sources:

Tyler Chin, "The Doctor is Outsourcing: To Hire or Not to Hire," *American Medical News*, August 11, 2003, www.ama-assn.org/amednews/2003/08/11/bisa0811.htm (accessed August 30, 2006).

Jennifer Clark, "MSO Increases Practice Revenues, Flexibility," *Cosmetic Surgery Times*, V. 8, No. 9, October 2005, search.ebscohost.com/login.aspx?direct=true&db=buh&AN=18430342&site=ehost-live (accessed August 30, 2006).

Fredrick A. Creighton, "Maximizing the Revenue Cycle Interface Between an Academic Group Practice and an Institutional-Based Management Services Organization (MSO)," ACMPE Professional Paper (Englewood, CO: American College of Medical Practice Executives, 2004).

CHAPTER 7

Professional Responsibility

QUESTION 80

I would like to pursue board certification with ACMPE, but it seems like a big commitment. How important is certification for medical practice administrators?

Attaining board certification through the American College of Medical Practice Executives (ACMPE) demonstrates a focus on and drive for excellence in medical practice management. Following the steps of advancement through the certification process will increase your knowledge and enhance your job performance. Certification and fellowship show a commitment to the profession and leadership responsibilities that is recognized by physicians and other industry professionals. The personal benefits of certification include confirming your knowledge in all the practice management subject domains and competencies and the knowledge of accomplishing the goal. New networking opportunities with other executives open up.

The additional benefits of being a Certified Medical Practice Executive (CMPE) include:

➤ Earning more, on average, than noncertified professionals (see table in "A Closer Look");

➤ Having a distinct competitive advantage over other candidates when seeking employment; and

➤ Being viewed by peers and employers as valued resources.

Source:

"Welcome to ACMPE," www.mgma.com/acmpe/index.cfm (accessed August 31, 2006).

A CLOSER LOOK...

Practice executive median compensation

Executive title	CMPE	Not affiliated with ACMPE
Chief executive officers of practices with 25 or fewer physicians	$150,000	$128,865
Chief executive officers of practices with 26 or more physicians	$234,148	$208,866
Practice administrators of practices with fewer than 7 physicians	$78,442	$72,000
Practice administrators of practices with 26 or more physicians	$164,668	$92,718
Practice administrators of practices with 7 to 25 physicians	$102,595	$92,273

Source: Medical Group Management Association, *Management Compensation Survey: 2005 Report Based on 2004 Data* (Englewood, CO: Medical Group Management Association, 2005).

ACMPE Certification Goes Over Big in One Organization

When it comes to administrator professional responsibility, Carolinas Physicians Network, Charlotte, N.C., sets the bar high. It is so high, in fact, that its leadership has an unwritten expectation that executives will strive to attain board certification through ACMPE and reach beyond that to become Fellows.

"If we are to succeed in this environment, we need to develop executives with group practice management experience," says J. Frederick Rice, FACMPE, senior vice president, Carolinas Physicians Network. "If you're going to be an executive in this company, you need to get your certification nailed down."

Rice and five of his executive colleagues in the organization are Fellows in ACMPE. They set the expectation for the 100 practice managers in the Carolinas HealthCare System that certification and Fellowship are the "best things you can do to advance in this company."

Source: Lisa H. Schneck, "Where the Fellows Rule," *MGMA Connexion*, V. 5, No. 8, September 2005.

QUESTION 81

What are the major factors in becoming a successful leader in medical practice management?

In many ways the keys to being a successful health care leader are the same as those for successful leaders in any field or setting. The characteristics identified in many leadership theories include the following:

➤ Strong personal ethics and integrity;

➤ Courage to do what needs to be done, regardless of the cost or risk to you or the company, and the courage to take risks after considering the potential rewards and ramifications;

➤ Vision of where you want to go, what you want to accomplish, what the organization's future should be, and the communication skills to bring them to life;

➤ Competence – that is, the knowledge and skills – to accomplish the job and lead others, but also the desire to continue to learn and grow;

➤ Passion about what you are doing;

➤ Effective communication in sharing knowledge and ideas and the desire to listen to others;

➤ Accountability in accepting responsibility for what you say and do;

➤ The ability to work with people, to understand them, accept them, and value their interests; and

➤ The ability to inspire and motivate others.

Many of these characteristics are part emotional intelligence. *Emotional intelligence* is identified as having the characteristics of self-awareness, self-regulation, motivation, empathy, and social skills. Some leadership studies have shown that emotional competence is a major factor in an individual's success in leadership positions. Like other types of competence, emotional intelligence can be developed and enhanced through practice and frequent application.

The complex challenges of the health care industry do require leaders with exceptional leadership skills and competencies. The Healthcare Leadership Alliance (HLA), a coalition of five health care professional societies, corroborated to define the leadership competencies in health care. The HLA Competency Directory can be used for self-assessments, the competencies of leadership teams, and leadership development programs.

The following are the five key domains and examples of the core competencies:

1. **Communication and relationship management**

    This domain focuses on the ability to communicate clearly and concisely with internal and external customers, establish and maintain relationships, and facilitate constructive interactions with individuals and groups. Knowledge competencies include:

    ➤ Organizational structure and relationships;

    ➤ Principles of communication and their applications (for example, crisis communication and alternative dispute resolution); and

    ➤ Public relations.

    Skill competencies include the ability to:

    ➤ Build collaborative relationships;

    ➤ Build effective physician and administrator leadership teams;

- Communicate organizational mission, vision, objectives, and priorities; and
- Create, participate in, and lead teams.

2. **Leadership**

    Leadership is the ability to facilitate motivation, create a shared vision, and lead an organization to success. The core knowledge-based competency that applies here is an understanding of leadership styles and techniques. Core skill-based competencies include the ability to:

    - Gain physician buy-in to accept risk and support new business ventures;
    - Advocate and participate in health care policy initiatives (for example, uninsured crisis, medical malpractice, access to health care, and patient safety);
    - Anticipate and plan strategies to overcome obstacles; and
    - Create an organizational climate that encourages teamwork.

3. **Professionalism**

    Professionalism is behavior that conforms with ethical and professional standards; it includes responsibility to the patient and community, service orientation, and a commitment to lifelong learning and improvement. Knowledge competencies related to professionalism are:

    - Organizational, business, and personal ethics;
    - Professional roles, responsibility, and accountability;

- Professional societies and memberships;
- Professional standards and codes of ethics;
- Time- and stress-management techniques; and
- Patients' rights and responsibilities.

4. **Knowledge of the health care environment**

   A successful leader must demonstrate an understanding of the health care system and the environment in which its managers and providers function. This domain encompasses a long list of core knowledge competencies, including:

   - Organization and delivery of health care;
   - Funding and payment mechanisms of the health care system;
   - Community standards of care;
   - Regulatory and administrative environment;
   - The patient's perspective; and
   - Health care technological research and advancements.

5. **Business knowledge and skills**

   Leaders in health care management should have the ability to apply basic business principles, including organizational and analytical thinking. These principles require skills in financial management, human resources management, strategic planning and marketing, information management, risk management, and quality improvement.

   The day in which only a chief financial officer needs to know about financial planning or only a chief information officer needs to know about information systems is gone. Out of 300 total knowledge and skill-based competencies, only 67 were defined as specialty. Most of those related to the distinct aspects of physician practice management. Yet even within this leadership domain, the vast majority of the competencies were deemed relevant across disciplines.

For the complete list of health care leadership competencies and to use the Microsoft® Excel-based tool, download the HLA Competency Directory from the HLA Website, www.healthcareleadershipalliance.org.

The five members of the Healthcare Leadership Alliance are:

- Medical Group Management Association and its certification body, the American College of Medical Practice Executives;
- American College of Healthcare Executives;
- American Organization of Nurse Executives;
- Healthcare Financial Management Association; and
- Healthcare Information and Management Systems Society.

Sources:

Vicki L. Ackerman, "Leadership: Success Through Character Development and Ethical Decisions," ACMPE Professional Paper (Englewood, CO: American College of Medical Practice Executives, 2004).

Pamela L. Lehman, "Emotional Intelligence and Career Success: A Crucial Evolution," *APA Matrix*, V. 17, No. 2, 2003.

"Impromptu: What Does it Take to Lead?" *MGMA Connexion*, V. 6, No. 4, April 2006.

QUESTION 82

How can I improve my public speaking and writing skills?

Excellent communication skills are among the identified traits important for successful leaders. Communicating face to face, in meetings, and by e-mail are important, but the challenge for most individuals is public speaking and professional writing. These skills are important not only for sharing what you need people to hear, but also because they affect how people perceive you.

It is possible to take courses and read the literature for ideas on how to improve your communication skills, but the most important skill-building technique is *practice*.

Writing skills frequently begin to fade after college, especially in today's age of communicating quickly through e-mail. Other people's perceptions of you are still influenced by your e-mail messages and reports, so it is important that these are written professionally. Means of maintaining and improving writing skills include:

➤ Writing in a journal, practicing business writing style;

FOR MORE INFORMATION...

Toastmasters

Toastmasters International (www.toastmasters.org) offers clubs that provide excellent opportunities to practice and improve your speaking. There are usually several groups in each community meeting at different times and locations. These clubs are exceptionally helpful because of the feedback and suggestions that participants provide to each other. You can also pick topics of personal interest that may be easier to present.

- Reviewing your e-mail messages and reports to ensure they are of the quality you demand for yourself;

- Having a professional editor or a friend whose writing style you respect review your work;

- Writing case studies or a research paper for ACMPE certification;

- Attending workshops on technical or professional writing skills; and

- Writing articles, essays, or professional papers and submitting them for publication.

This last option does not have to be only in professional publications; you can write materials on personal interests and hobbies. However, writing articles for professional journals will broaden your writing skills, enhance your recognition in your field, and help in advancing the profession.

Public speaking skills are also vital to leaders. These skills enable one to speak more effectively in staff meetings, in front of the board, or at professional meetings. Practice, practice, and more practice will improve your skills.

As with writing skills, speaking skills can be developed, and you can contribute to the profession by offering to give presentations at local association meetings, at hospital-based or other community events, or even at national events.

Professional speakers offer several tips for successful presentations:

- Allow adequate time to prepare and organize your speech;

- Understand your audience and their expectations;

- Rehearse the speech beforehand in front of friends or a mirror, with your family, or in the woods;

- ➤ Look confident and happy (looking that way will help you feel that way);

- ➤ Arrive at the location at least 30 minutes early and familiarize yourself with the setup and sound system;

- ➤ Speak with the appropriate speed so that listeners can stay attentive and follow the speech;

- ➤ Use pauses, voice inflections, humor, and stories to add interest and emphasis to your speech;

- ➤ Pay attention to your body language – maintain eye contact, use natural gestures to emphasize points, and don't pace or move nervously; and

- ➤ Pay attention to your breathing.

Sources:

Kathy Kerchner, "Preparing for Better Presentations," *Public Relations Tactics*, V. 11, No. 2, February 2004.

Barbara Linney, "Presentations That Hold You Spellbound," *Physician Executive*, V. 26, No. 5, September 2005.

Ronald Menaker, "Know How: Write Power: Using a Journal for Professional Development," *MGMA Connexion*, V. 2, No. 4, April 2002.

QUESTION 83

What steps can I take to ensure my continued professional growth?

Professional growth is an ongoing process, not an end unto itself. The cycle consists of personal assessment, knowledge acquisition, and execution. A variety of tools are available to help at each step.

Assess your knowledge and skills in medical practice management. What competencies and knowledge areas are you strong in and which require knowledge building? The following tools are based on the ACMPE Body of Knowledge for Medical Practice Management:

- ➤ The ACMPE Technical/Professional Knowledge Inventory for a subjective evaluation of your knowledge of key medical practice areas;

- ➤ The ACMPE Knowledge Assessment for a comprehensive objective assessment; and

- ➤ The HLA Competency Directory tool at the HLA Website, www.healthcareleadershipalliance.org.

Acquire knowledge about medical practice management and general business theories and principles. Locate opportunities to fill in the gaps identified by the above assessments. Recognize that the medical practice management field is not standing still, and you need to learn and grow with it. Resources include books, articles, audioconferences, seminars, and university programs. Be sure to explore sources beyond the practice management field.

If you become a Certified Medical Practice Executive, you will be recognized as knowledgeable and committed to the profession. The recognition will open additional opportunities to you (see Question #80).

Excel in the field by continuing your learning, identifying opportunities for achieving excellence, guiding and mentoring others, and contributing to the field and the community.

At every step in your professional development, you should identify a mentor, coach, or guide who can help you grow. This individual may be a senior manager in your organization or in another organization, a respected peer or friend, or a professional management coach. The mentor should help you critically assess the professional decisions you have made, offer constructive feedback on your performance, provide new insights, and help you tap into your personal strengths.

Professional growth occurs when you take on new challenges and opportunities. Stagnation occurs if you fail to grow or stay in the same position. If new opportunities are not offered to you, look for them. Even becoming a mentor to a younger professional will help you grow as you help someone else grow.

Sources:

Christina Pope, "Defining the Profession: Stepping Stones: Assess, Learn, Certify and Excel on Your Pathway to Professional Development," *MGMA Connexion*, V. 5, No. 10, November 2005.

Bob Redling, "Defining the Profession: How Am I Doing, Coach? A Mentor Can Help You Develop Your Potential," *MGMA Connexion*, V. 3, No. 10, November 2003.

I recently accepted the position of practice administrator, but it's taking over my life. How can I maintain balance between my personal and professional lives and avoid burnout?

Congratulations on recognizing your stress before you reach burnout. It is important to recognize that you are not alone; many of your peers are dealing with the same issue. Practice administrators are in stressful positions – trying to meet or exceed physician expectations and demands, supporting staff and handling their issues, and managing an endless list of responsibilities.

Managed or controlled stress can be beneficial, driving us to accomplish our goals and challenges. Constant uncontrolled stress over many months and years, however, is unhealthy and can affect job performance. There are steps you can take to manage the stress and rescue your life.

You've already taken the first vital step in recognizing the symptoms of excessive stress. Because you are relatively new to the position, your stress is probably at its highest level as you learn your new responsibilities, make decisions on issues for the first time, and are getting to know the practice and its physicians and employees. As time passes, the job may get easier and the stress may lessen – or they may not.

Because of your position as an administrator, your stress will never go away. What you can learn now about controlling it will benefit you through the remainder of your career.

Recognize that you have many demands on your time: the responsibilities of your position, being with your family, and taking care of yourself. The most important of the three is taking care of yourself, because without that you can't take care of the other demands. Remember to get enough sleep, eat healthy, exercise, and take time to relax – these are the things that make you feel better. You also should assess your personal life to determine if it is a source of additional stressors and how you can best address them. Talk with a family member or friend about the stress and how to relieve it, not relive it.

On the job there are additional steps you can take to regain control of your life:

> ➤ **Develop a list of priorities, and determine what must be done and when.** Have you been spending time on the highest priorities, or have you been tackling other less important projects, leaving you with the stress of the higher priorities weighing on you?
>
> ➤ **Determine which tasks can be delegated to others.** New managers frequently think they must take care of everything. Your staff members are qualified or can be trained to take on additional responsibilities. They may have even handled some already while your position was vacant.
>
> ➤ **Focus on what you can control.** You may be worrying over factors, both inside work and out, that you have no control over. Concentrate on what you can change and what needs to be changed.
>
> ➤ **Be creative in seeking solutions.** Don't feel that you must do something the way it was done before or the way you want it done if it's not working. Be flexible

and remember that the best solutions may come from someone else;

➤ **Set limits.** Don't allow your job to take over your life. Set a reasonable schedule for work and stick to it. Don't take work home every night and weekend.

➤ **Take an occasional mental break.** Try 10 to 15 minutes of deep breathing, meditation, or exercise to get away from the stressors. Catch your breath and start anew.

➤ **Take your scheduled vacation time.** You will need that time to refresh and recharge.

➤ **Communicate.** All too often external factors stress us, and rather than communicating their affect on us, we keep it bottled up inside – adding to our general level of stress. And don't be afraid to deliver bad news – sooner rather than later!

QUESTION 85

I am looking for information or a template for a code of conduct or a code of ethics for employee, administrator, and physician behavior in a medical practice. Where can I find some examples?

Codes of conduct and codes of ethics clarify for employees, management, and external stakeholders the standards that shape the organization's behavior and decision making. The code is important for specifying behavioral norms within the organization, compliance with regulations, and the ethical values in organizational and individual behaviors.

Your practice's board or governing group, along with the president or managing partner, need to take the lead in developing your code of conduct. Their buy-in and commitment to the code are needed to ensure their compliance in decision making and to ensure that other physicians and employees understand the importance of complying with the code. Staff representatives should also be included in the development process as well – you will need their buy-in, too.

> **KEY POINT**
>
>  *Codes of conduct and codes of ethics are important for specifying behavioral norms within the organization, compliance with regulations, and the ethical values in organizational and individual behaviors.*

You can use codes of conduct from other sources as a basis, but your code must be written to the specifics of your practice and its mission and vision. Specific codes may be needed for employees, physicians, and the board. See "For More Information" for sources of sample codes of conduct.

A study of codes of conduct from U.S. and international companies identified many similarities. They typically included recognition of and provisions for the stakeholders of the organization: patients, the community, employees, competitors, and partners/suppliers. Other similarities were found in the following principles and their content:

➤ **The Fiduciary Principle** – Employees and managers have responsibility for the financial well-being of the organization. This principle includes provisions for disclosing conflicts of interest and not benefiting oneself over the interests of the organization.

➤ **Property Principle** – Statements prohibit theft and embezzlement, and they require the respect of

FOR MORE INFORMATION...

Sources for sample codes of conduct or ethics:

✔ American Medical Association's Code of Medical Ethics (www.ama-assn.org);

✔ MGMA's and ACMPE's Code of Ethics (www.mgma.com);

✔ Literature and Websites on the topic, including the Center for the Study of Ethics in the Professions, Illinois Institute of Technology (www.iit.edu/departments/csep/PublicWWW/codes);

✔ Samples that your peers are willing to share;

✔ MGMA's *Information Exchange* #6673, "Physicians – Service Guidelines and Code of Conduct";

✔ MGMA's "Physician Orientation" *Information Exchange* #6247, which includes a sample code of conduct from a medical practice; and

✔ *Governing Policies Manual for Medical Practices,* by Alys Novak, MBA (Englewood, CO: Medical Group Management Association, 1996).

---

personal and business property, as well as intellectual property.

➤ **Reliability Principle** – Individuals agree to keep promises, fulfill contracts, work agreed-upon hours, and complete their commitments.

➤ **Honesty or Truth Principle** – Individuals agree to be honest, not to deceive with misinformation, and not to commit fraud.

➤ **Dignity Principle** – Actions and decisions are based on the concern for others (employees, patients, and the community) and their health, safety, privacy, and self-esteem.

> **Fairness Principle** – All employees, patients, and other stakeholders will be treated fairly. Differential treatment and discrimination is not allowed.

> **Citizenship Principle** – Individuals will exhibit appropriate behavior as a citizen within the organization and the community to encourage excellence and continued well-being of the organization and the community. Examples include participating in committees, community-building events, and governance.

These principles apply to medical practices and can be customized to meet the specifics of the industry and its professions. Statements addressing compliance with Medicare fraud and abuse regulations and HIPAA privacy regulations help protect the organization against possible infractions and audits. Statements regarding dignity, fairness, and other principles guide physicians and others in appropriate relations and behavior toward others.

Once the leadership and key stakeholders have completed the code, it should be distributed for review and discussion. Participants should understand the importance of the document and that compliance is expected. All employees and physicians should sign it. Physicians should realize that they are expected to comply and are not exempted because of their position. If an employee, physician, or leader breaks the code, s/he should be held accountable and face consequences commiserate with the infraction.

Sources:

Mary Jane Kornacki and Jack Silversin, "Creating a Physician Compact that Drives Group Success," *MGM Journal*, V. 47, No. 3, May 2000.

Lynn Paine, Rohit Deshpande, and Joshua D. Margolis, "Up to Code," *Harvard Business Review*, V. 83, No. 12, December 2005.

Richard E. Thompson, "Misbehaving Physicians and Professional Ethics," *Physician Executive*, V. 30, No. 5, September/October 2004.

QUESTION 86

I'm tired of people in Washington, D.C., and the state capitol making decisions without understanding the impact on health care organizations. What can I do to influence the lawmaking bodies that affect my practice?

It is important for medical practice executives to speak out on legislative and regulatory issues that affect the industry. Legislators and policy makers hear frequently from health care corporations, but they need to hear the perspective of physicians, practice executives, and their patients. You should encourage action on issues that will improve patient care and practice management as often as you speak out against legislation.

The MGMA Government Affairs Department offers several tips on how executives and physicians can advocate for legislation and policies that benefit medical practices and ambulatory patient care:

➤ Keep informed about the issues. Read updates from the MGMA Government Affairs Department, local and national medical societies, and other sources. Review what you read critically to understand the context of the issues and their full implications.

➤ Take grassroots action. Request the introduction of a bill and identify a sponsor and cosponsor, educate the legislators and policy makers about the bill and its benefits, and rally support from your peers.

➤ Write letters expressing approval or disapproval and educating the representatives about the impact of pertinent bills. Also, write letters to thank representatives when you agree with their votes.

➤ Meet with your representatives or their staff in their district offices or in Washington, D.C.

➤ Telephone your lawmakers, especially in rapidly evolving situations. Follow up with a visit or letter.

➤ Attend educational programs on legislative issues and grassroots lobbying.

➤ Encourage your local associations to sponsor advocacy programs and days to meet with legislators.

➤ Work closely with your state MGMA and local affiliates to develop an active government affairs committee.

Sources:

Christina Pope, "The Learning Curve: View from the Medicare Fray: MDs are MIA," *MGMA e-Connexion,* April 2004.

Medical Group Management Association Government Affairs Department, "Democracy in Action: A Guide for Grassroots Advocacy," www.mgma.com/members/advocacy/grassroots.cfm (accessed September 2, 2006).

QUESTION 87

I'm dealing with an ethical dilemma and need some advice. The physician owner of the practice wants to increase his income by reducing employees' medical benefits. I disagree with him. How do I deal with this situation?

Practice executives do have a professional and personal commitment to make ethical decisions and act in an ethical manner. Competencies and skills identified in the ACMPE Body of Knowledge for Medical Practice Executives include the following:

➤ Developing a personal code of ethics;

➤ Explaining the importance of ethical considerations as part of the organization's decision-making process; and

➤ Advocating for ethical decision making in the practice.

The difficulty is in knowing how to proceed when an ethical issue arises.

The first step is to determine whether the situation is indeed an ethical dilemma or if it can be resolved with a financial or cost–benefit analysis. As for your specific ethical dilemma, consider taking the following action:

➤ Gather data to determine if the physician's income and production is higher or lower than similar physicians. Is there a reason for the physician to be concerned about his income? Is he greedy? You don't need to show comparative compensation figures to the physician, but you do need to know where he stands compared to his peers.

➤ Be sure to work with your state MGMA and local affiliates to gather local market information as well.

➤ Compare the current employee medical benefits with industry standards. Are they higher than average? Many businesses are modifying employee benefits as cost-cutting measures and requiring employees to invest more of their own funds in their health care. If benefits are already low, has it caused increased turnover or difficulty in hiring the best candidates? Will lowering benefits cause more turnover or hiring difficulties?

➤ Study the practice financials and evaluate additional revenue ideas. Is it possible to reduce expenses elsewhere? Can additional revenue be found that will offset the benefits expenses?

➤ Does the practice have a code of conduct, a code of ethics, or other document that can support your position?

After you have gathered the data and are ready to present it, meet with the physician owner to discuss the issue and present your ideas. Show the potential financial consequences for the change (in this case, increased turnover, lower employee morale, and the costs for replacing employees). Express your ideas for achieving the requested change in an ethical manner. Demonstrate that the decision runs contrary to the practice's code of conduct, mission statement, or other documents.

Is there an ally, such as another physician or individual the physician respects, who will understand the dilemma of the physician owner's decision and can help you? Can you present your case to a governing board?

If the physician insists on proceeding with his idea, which you feel is unethical, your options may be to refuse to implement the decision (possibly leading to your termination) or to submit your resignation in protest. Neither decision will be easy for you, but you will know that you will have complied with your own professional and personal ethics.

The above discussion is just one example of the many potentially ethical dilemmas that practice executives face. The steps taken in handling the dilemma (gathering data, assessing the situation, presenting your case, and making the final decision) will be similar no matter what the situation is. The decisions will be easier if you remember to stick to your core values and your professional and personal code of ethics.

Source:
Christina Pope, "Defining the Profession: Do the Right Thing: Why Even Well-Intentioned Administrators Need a Professional Responsibility," *MGMA Connexion*, V. 5, No. 8, September 2005.

CHAPTER 8

Risk Management

QUESTION

What are the regulations regarding translator or interpreter requirements in group practices? Do I have to offer this service?

For deaf or hearing-impaired patients, Title III of the Americans with Disabilities Act (ADA) requires places of public accommodation, including medical practice offices, to "furnish appropriate auxiliary aids and services where necessary to ensure effective communication with individuals with disabilities." Health care facilities must cover the cost of auxiliary aids and services to ensure effective communication, unless doing so would cause an "undue burden" in effort or expense.

Aids and services can mean qualified interpreters, note takers, computer-aided transcription services, audio recordings, and other methods. When gestures and using a notepad will not suffice during a clinical or other visit, the medical practice will have to hire a qualified interpreter. ADA guidelines prohibit family members and friends from providing interpretation for patients. The regulation defines a qualified interpreter as a person "who is able to interpret effectively, accurately and impartially, both receptively and expressively, using any necessary specialized vocabulary." Thus, emotional involvement and issues of confidentiality may prevent someone close to the patient from providing objective service.

Practices can comply with the regulation by hiring an interpreter, having a qualified staff member qualified to interpret, or using computer-assisted real-time transcription (CART), a service in which an operator types what is said into a computer that displays the words on a screen.

FOR MORE INFORMATION...

Internet resources:

✔ www.atanet.org — The American Translators Association Website offers accreditation services and a database of accredited translators and interpreters.

✔ www.hhs.gov/ocr/lep — This Website of the U.S. Department of Health and Human Services includes the full text of the limited English proficiency (LEP) law. The site also provides suggestions on serving LEP patients.

For patients with limited knowledge of English, you are required to supply free interpreters and appropriate forms during patient encounters, regardless of their insurance, if you receive funds from Medicaid, Medicare Part A, or the State Children's Health Insurance Program. The limited English proficiency (LEP) guidelines, published by the U.S. Department of Health and Human Services, Office of Civil Rights, state: "Recipient/covered entities must take steps to ensure that LEP persons who are eligible for their programs or services have meaningful access to the health and social service benefits that they provide. The most important step ... is to provide the language assistance necessary to ensure such access, at no cost to the LEP person."

Options for providing translating services include:

➤ Hiring bilingual staff members;

➤ Training your existing staff in foreign languages;

➤ Hiring an interpreter on a contract or full-time basis, depending on your need. You might be able to use community volunteers, rather than expensive interpreters; or

➤ Using telephone interpretation services. These services charge by the minute and can be more affordable than in-person interpreters.

Sources:

Ariana Harner, "Know-How: Speak Words of Health: Providing Care to Patients with Limited English Proficiency," *MGMA Connexion*, V. 2, No. 10, November/December 2002, www3.mgma.com/articles/index.cfm?fuseaction=detail.main&articleID=12245 (accessed August 8, 2006).

Lisa H. Schneck, "Know-How: Now Hear This: Practices Must Provide Interpretive Services for Deaf and Hearing-Impaired Patients," *MGMA Connexion*, V. 4, No. 9, October 2004, www3.mgma.com/articles/index.cfm?fuseaction=detail.main&articleID=13078 (accessed August 8, 2006).

One of our physicians has approached me about dismissing a noncompliant patient. What are the proper legal and ethical considerations in dismissing patients from a practice?

Every group practice administrator eventually deals with the question of whether and how to dismiss a difficult patient from the practice. Problematic patients are those who are abusive, threatening, offensive, or noncompliant. If dismissed, the patient will have to identify an alternative source of care.

Dismissing a patient from a group practice has legal and ethical implications. Because every state has its own laws and regulations, confer with your legal counsel and state medical board to make sure you comply with legal provisions and community norms. It is critical that your practice avoid the possibility of a charge of patient abandonment. Further, decisions based on race, gender, sexual preference, or religious affiliation violate federal law.

Prior to dismissing a patient, your practice should:

➤ Already have developed a group policy and approach to patient dismissal;

A CLOSER LOOK...

Reasons for patient dismissal from a practice

Noncompliance	94%
Nonpayment	62%
Other	32%
Litigation	30%

Note: The percentages total more than 100 percent because respondents could select more than one option.

Source: Medical Group Management Association, "Patient Discharge/Termination of Care," *Information Exchange* #4029 (Englewood, CO: Medical Group Management Association, 2004).

➤ On the patient's chart, clearly document the problem behavior and discussions with the patient about the issue;

➤ Record efforts to educate the patient, attempts to help him or her change the behavior, and explanations of the consequences if change does not occur;

➤ Consult with a legal advisor to ensure compliance with legal and regulatory mandates; and

➤ Follow a formal patient notification process.

The notification process should include a letter, reviewed first by legal counsel and sent by certified mail (return receipt requested), that advises the patient to find another physician within 30 days. The letter should explain the reasons for the decision and give a brief history of events. The letter should state that the group will continue to provide care to the patient for 30 days and asks the patient to provide the name of a new physician so that the practice can forward copies of the patient's medical records. If receipt of the letter is acknowledged but the patient does not respond, you should send a follow-up letter 15 days before the deadline that reiterates the terms of the original letter and the impending deadline.

Source:

Hobart Collins, "Begone with You: Dismissing Problem Patients from Your Practice, *MGMA Connexion*, V. 3, No. 5, May 2003, www3.mgma.com/articles/index.cfm?fuseaction=detail.main&articleID=12465 (accessed August 8, 2006).

Prior to proceeding further with a proposed joint venture, I'd like to know more about Stark regulations and joint ventures. What information do you have?

Medical practices should be wary of entering into joint ventures because of the Stark regulations and other laws affecting physician referral and financial relationships. Stark regulations accept financial and referral arrangements within group practices, but regulators are suspicious of joint ventures between physician groups.

The Stark law declares that joint ventures involving designated health services are illegal unless covered by one of these exceptions:

➤ The facilities are in a rural area;

➤ Arrangements are between an employer and an employee;

➤ Joint ventures involve groups of radiologists, pathologists, or radiation oncologists; and

➤ Agreements involve publicly held securities as defined in the Stark law.

A safe harbor was established by the Office of Inspector General, protecting physician groups that form certain joint ventures if they adhere to strict, narrow guidelines of the rules. A physician can refer Medicare patients to a large entity that is a part of a large corporation in which s/he owns shares. For example, there is a safe harbor for physicians who self-refer to a small entity in which no more than 40 percent of the facility is owned by potentially referring physician owners and no more than 40 percent of its revenue is generated by investors. Referral volume can't be a factor in determining return on investment or else the exemption is lost. The investment return must be based only on the amount invested. Also, nonreferring physician investors must be offered investment opportunities on terms equal to those of the referring investors. The facility cannot make a loan (or guarantee) that allows the physician to acquire his or her interest. Finally, the clinic cannot offer services to physician-investors on terms better than noninvestors. Investments totaling less than the 40 percent threshold are acceptable.

The overarching rule in federal regulations is that joint ventures must be created for legitimate purposes. Acceptable reasons to form a joint venture include to aggregate capital to purchase equipment or to spread risk in connection with a new service. When a joint venture involves little more than a reconfiguration of the names and dollars in an existing service line, regulators may question its legitimacy and legal compliance.

Sources:

Ed Bryant, "Capital Financing for Physician Group Practices," in Lawrence F. Wolper, MBA, FACMPE, ed., *Physician Practice Management: Essential Operational and Financial Knowledge* (Sudbury, MA: Jones and Bartlett Publishers, 2005), pp. 660-661.

Marline Kesgard Ptacnik, "How Stark Rules and Regulations Impact Health Systems," ACMPE Professional Paper (Englewood, CO: American College of Medical Practice Executives, September 2005).

Bruce A. Johnson, "Reading the Tea Leaves: Making Sense of New Legal Guidance on Ancillary Services," *MGMA Connexion*, V. 5, No. 6, July 2005, www3.mgma.com/articles/index.cfm?fuseaction=detail.main&articleID=13427 (accessed August 10, 2006).

QUESTION 91

How do I ensure that all of my employees are adequately trained on HIPAA requirements?

Medical practices and other health care organizations are required to maintain an effective Health Insurance Portability and Accountability Act of 1996 (HIPAA) compliance program. Conducting staff training ensures a corporate culture of compliance with the privacy regulations. The U.S. Sentencing Commission indicates that "the organization must have taken steps to communicate effectively its standards and procedures to all employees and other agents, by requiring participation in training programs or by disseminating publications that explain in a practical manner what is required." To ensure compliance, your training must be provided on an ongoing basis with periodic updates.

Your practice's HIPAA compliance policies must describe your training program, specific subjects to be covered in the training, and the frequency of the training. The policy should also specify consequences for not completing the training and not following the compliance policy and HIPAA privacy regulations. Document each training session, including what was covered and who participated. Set up a system so that every staff member receives training. Keep these materials with your program materials.

If you are using a product for your HIPAA training, it should include a form or checklist to record employee training. The training product may also include a sample quiz or test for employees. You can also use a privacy policy training checklist. One good example can be found in Chapter 17 of MGMA's *Operating Policies & Procedures Manual for Medical Practices,* 3rd Edition.

The training can be modified for groups of employees, depending on their roles with patients and protected health

> **KEY POINT**
>
>  Your HIPAA compliance policies must describe your training program, the subjects covered, and the frequency of the training. The policy should specify consequences for not completing the training and not following the compliance policy and HIPAA privacy regulations.

information. Your front desk staff will need to be trained on the Notice of Privacy Practices and Acknowledgement Process. The medical records staff will need to be trained on the new authorization and minimum necessary requirement. Clinical staff will also need to be trained on the minimum necessary requirement, as well as raising their level of consciousness about incidental disclosures.

Sources:

John S. Cunningham, "Corporate Compliance: The Legal and Ethical Operations of Physician Group Practices," ACMPE Professional Paper (Englewood, CO: American College of Medical Practice Executives, June 2006).

Nancy M. Enos, "Preparing the Medical Practice for HIPAA Privacy Compliance," ACMPE Professional Paper (Englewood, CO: American College of Medical Practice Executives, July 2003).

United States Sentencing Commission (May 1, 2004), "Proposed Amendments to Chapter 8" (Electronic Version), *Organizational Guidelines and Compliance,* www.ussc.gov/orgguide.HTM (accessed August 11, 2006).

QUESTION 92

I'm looking for guidelines or suggestions on dealing with courtesy discounts for employees who are seen by the physician in the clinic. Is it appropriate to write off copays? Are an employee's dependents allowed to have the discounts?

The U.S. Department of Health and Human Services Office of Inspector General (OIG) does look closely at medical practice courtesy discounts to ensure there is no violation of federal regulations. The OIG Compliance Guidance for Small Group Practices defines *professional courtesy* as either:

➤ A physician waiving all or a part of the fee for services provided to the physician's office staff, other physicians, and/or their families; or

➤ Waiving copayment or other out-of-pocket expenses for physicians, employees, and their families.

Two circumstances can create a violation, according to OIG. The first circumstance is providing discounts to referring physicians or their families, which could be considered a violation of antikickback regulations. The second circumstance is discounting fees or waiving copayments for employees or their family members who are receiving federal health care benefits (such as Medicare, Medicaid, or other federal program). This conflicts with the anti-inducement law, which limits providing gifts and free services to beneficiaries unless the patients are financially needy or to promote the acceptance of certain preventive health services.

If the above two circumstances do not exist, providing employees and their dependents courtesy discounts should be acceptable in terms of federal regulations. However, there may be state regulations or health plan contract terms that

A CLOSER LOOK...

OIG areas of concern:

✔ A physician's practice of extending professional courtesy by waiving the entire fee or copayment for a group of persons in a manner that may generate federal health care program business for the physician; and

✔ Waiver of copayment for a federal health care program beneficiary who is not financially needy.

do prohibit offering discounts or waiving copayments. You should understand your state laws and the plans' contracts prior to offering courtesy discounts.

Sources:

Robert M. Portman, "Professional Courtesy: Illegal Fraud or Innocent Favor?" *Administrative Eyecare*, V. 12, No. 1, Winter 2003.

OIG Compliance Program for Individual and Small Group Practices, *Federal Register* 65 (2000), pp. 59434-59447.

QUESTION 93

One of my performance goals this year is to develop a disaster and recovery plan. Are there any samples or suggestions on what should be included?

Practices face a variety of disasters that can threaten loss of property, medical and business records, financial well-being, and even human lives. Developing a comprehensive disaster and recovery plan and communicating the plan with staff will limit loss and speed recovery after a disaster.

MGMA member Thomas P. Peterson, MBA, FACMPE, offers the following checklist in developing a disaster plan:

❑ **Patient safety**

> ➤ Does the medical group have detailed evacuation plans? Has it carried out practice drills with staff, using people simulating patients with various stages of mobility?

> ➤ Have you designated responsibility for ensuring the practice's evacuation and securing the premises? If the power goes off, can you complete appropriate medical procedures, or do you need to establish backup power systems? How will you evacuate patients if the elevators stop working?

- Do you have a health care contingency plan developed with other providers, clinics, and hospitals – including emergency departments – to accept the practice's patients?

- Do you have a plan that balances medical supply inventories with vendor delivery capability during local, regional, or national emergencies?

❑ **Employee security**

- Have you designated an off-site location for employees (physicians and staff) to meet following an emergency?

- Physicians and staff members worrying about loved ones will not function effectively during a crisis. Do you have a plan for the safety of employees' families?

- Have you developed a chain of command that anticipates the loss of key personnel? Do employees understand their roles in an emergency? Do employees know who will step up to assist management?

- Do managers and supervisors know their roles in tracking employees and patients during an emergency?

- Have you identified counselors to help employees deal with the aftermath of a crisis?

❑ **Practice finances**

- Are the practice's finances all in one financial institution? If your bank is forced to close for a while, do you have a backup plan?

- How will you handle payroll, payments, and collections if the banking system shuts down?

- Does the practice have a safe to hold cash deposits while financial institutions are closed?
- Are duplicate financial records stored off-site?
- Have you designated backup personnel who can obtain off-site records if key personnel are lost?
- Have you taken steps to provide partial compensation to employees?

❑ **Practice capability**

- If patient charts are destroyed, do you have backup records off-site? Can you readily access records for patients with chronic illnesses or complicated treatment plans?
- Have you designated a spokesperson for the practice? Has s/he simulated scenarios that would require responses to the press and other interested parties?
- What is the role of the practice within the local community disaster plan? Have you trained key personnel to react properly?
- Is the practice prepared to respond to public health outbreaks that might put employees and patients at risk for life-threatening illnesses?
- Have you developed plans for practice downtime? How rapidly could you establish a temporary clinic?
- Do you have arrangements to duplicate the practice computer system while a destroyed system is being replaced or rebuilt?
- If you are using an electronic health record (EHR) system, do you have plans and capabili-

ties of accessing clinical information during power outages and other natural disasters?

➢ Does the practice store employee computer passwords and access codes off-site?

➢ What items, if any, should be removed during an evacuation of the practice, and who is responsible?

Recovering from a disaster can be simplified if recommendations in the disaster checklist are followed; however, it will never be an easy process. Practices that have recovered from recent disasters offer some valuable ideas:

➤ Communicate with the staff early and frequently, including about planned closings of the practice. Maintain a list of home and cell phone numbers for contacting employees and use a phone tree to simplify contacts.

➤ Set up a voice-mail recording that you can update remotely so employees can get current information.

➤ Be understanding of employees' needs, particularly if they have suffered property loss or need to care for family members.

➤ If there is time during the disaster, back up the EHR system, patient information, and other clinical and business systems prior to shutting them down. Otherwise, rely on regular backups stored off-site.

➤ Use an uninterrupted power supply (such as batteries or an emergency generator) to supply the EHR and phone systems.

➤ Use photo ID badges for staff returning to the facility, eliminating confusion from National Guard and other law enforcement agencies.

➤ Prepare for post-traumatic stress disorder among employees. Encourage use of the practice's Employee Assistance Program benefit or community services.

Sources:

Thomas P. Peterson, MBA, FACMPE. "Know-How: Be Prepared: A Checklist to Help Ready Your Practice for an Emergency," *MGMA Connexion*, V. 2, No. 1, January 2002, www3.mgma.com/articles/index.cfm?fuseaction=detail.main&articleID=11928 (accessed August 10, 2006).

Frederic R. Simmons, "Stormy Weather: Preparing for and Recovering from Disasters," *MGMA Connexion*, V. 6, No. 1, January 2006, www3.mgma.com/articles/index.cfm?fuseaction=detail.main&articleID=13656 (accessed August 10, 2006).

The group's board is interested in establishing a peer review process to address patient care concerns, coding issues, and compliance matters. What resources are there to help me set one up?

Hospital and managed care organizations' peer review processes have received a bad reputation. Physicians have accused these organizations of trying to dictate care delivery, being biased toward higher hospital users, and weeding out physicians who complain.

This reputation may cause physicians in your group to distrust the implementation of a peer review process. Peer review in medical practices can serve a legitimate and valuable purpose if the intent is to improve the quality of care and reduce the probability of litigation. It will not be successful, however, if the intent is to punish physicians. As you introduce the concept of peer review to your physicians, make sure that it is being developed for the right reasons and openly discuss these reasons.

The peer review process can be used to:

➤ Analyze the groups' success in following standard practice protocols – for example, protocols related to treating cardiac patients;

- Review medical documentation to ensure completion and accuracy, which will reduce the possibility of litigation;

- Identify medical errors and the means of reducing them;

- Compare productivity benchmarks to improve the organization's productivity; and

- Assess patient outcomes and opportunities for improvement.

Several states have implemented regulations affecting peer review. These regulations typically deal with hospital and/or managed care, but the regulations in your state should be reviewed to ensure compliance prior to developing your process.

The steps to establishing a peer review process are as follows:

1. Discuss the reasons for implementing the process, why it is important, and what the intended outcomes are. Develop goals for the peer review and encourage your managers and physicians to buy in to it.

2. Determine whether there will be a peer review committee or individual reviewers. Medical directors, quality-of-care staff, or other physicians or employees sometimes serve as the lead in the review process. If a committee is formed, identify who will serve on it and for how long. Even if individual reviewers are used, there should be the option of transferring issues of concern to a peer review, quality control, or similar committee.

3. Identify what information will be reviewed. Select control indicators and what standards will be used for benchmarking the group's data.

A CLOSER LOOK...

Survey of MGMA Members About Peer Review Committees

Who serves as peer review committee members?

Classification	Percent of respondents
Physician	85.4%
Board member	36.6%
President	26.8%
Medical director	22.0%
Attorney	7.3%
Other	39.0%

What is the primary focus of the peer review committee meeting?

Focus	Percent of respondents
Physicians' medical records for quality	85.7%
Patient complaints	61.9%
Medical outcomes	54.8%
Physician attitude/discipline	42.9%
Malpractice charges	23.8%
Impaired physicians	14.3%
Other	11.9%

Source: Medical Group Management Association, "Peer Review Committee," *Information Exchange* #3340 (Englewood, CO: Medical Group Management Association, 2004).

---

4. Set up processes for reporting the results and implementing changes. Remember that peer review provides an opportunity to identify areas of improvement.

5. Develop a schedule. The committee should meet on a regular basis to ensure timely review, but with the

option of meeting more often if an important issue needs to be addressed.

6. Periodically review the process with the group's leaders and physicians to determine if it is meeting its objectives or if it should be improved.

Sources

Kelly Johnson, "Development and Implementation of an External Peer-Review Process," *Journal of Healthcare Management*, V. 50, No. 2, March/April 2005.

"Outpatient Settings Can Avoid Inpatient Peer Review Mistakes," *Credentialing Across the Continuum*, September 2000.

Tallien R. Perry and Lynsey A. Mitchel, "What Every Executive, Compliance Officer, and In-House Counsel Needs to Know About State Laws Governing Peer Review in Managed Care Plans," *Journal of Health Care Compliance*, V. 8, No. 1, January/February 2006.

Our malpractice premiums are too high. What are other practices doing to reduce the costs of malpractice liability insurance?

There are several options, with varying risks and benefits for obtaining malpractice liability coverage. Physician-owned malpractice insurers have become increasingly popular because they are viewed as sympathetic to physicians. These companies exist in a number of forms; which form works best for your group will depend largely on the state where you practice, the size of your group, your medical specialties, the claims history of your physicians, and the types of coverage available.

Physician stock companies are traditionally organized by state medical societies as medical-liability-only companies owned by physicians and operating in a single state. Physician stock companies usually provide malpractice coverage for any and all medical specialties. They have a responsibility to report and return profits to investors.

Physician mutual companies merge the roles of policyholder and owner by having the insured physicians purchase stock in the company. This helps align goals, and physicians perceive the companies as being the most sympathetic. However, it may be more difficult for physicians to gauge an insurer's financial status without the reporting requirements of public stock companies. Mismanagement can cause the physician owners to lose twice: as stockholders experiencing decreased (or nonexistent) value for the shares and as policyholders who may not have coverage for claims.

Reciprocal insurers are structured like mutual companies, but they are not incorporated and, thus, lack capital. They retain individual accounts of the paid premiums. Expenses are debited to those accounts. An "attorney in fact" manages the organization and the funds. One benefit is that the individual does not assume risk for others in the pool. The disadvantage is that there is no real insurance, or risk-pooling, element, and a significantly large claim or two can affect the insurer's account balance. Reinsurance or high-deductible primary insurance offers an option on an individual or group basis.

Physician trusts, also not incorporated, assess members for premiums after expenses, as well as policyholder claims. Physician trusts don't charge individuals up front for things that may never happen, but they may undergo greater premium volatility without reserves set aside for spikes in claims frequency or severity.

Risk retention groups (RRGs) are not really insurance companies, but they provide a mechanism for obtaining insurance. RRGs may practice in multiple states but fall under insurance laws only in the home state. Groups of similar physicians, such as anesthesiologists, purchase coverage from an existing carrier. If conflicts with management arise, the group may move en masse to another insurer.

Insurance captives involve large groups of physicians that pool resources to cover administrative costs and perhaps pool risk to cover an initial amount of liability for each physician. Typically, physicians purchase reinsurance to cover excess losses of the captive. Physician members must pay management fees for adjudication of claims and reserves, defense counsel, and so on. In essence, insurance captives are the medical malpractice liability cousins of self-insured health insurance plans. Like them, the more people in the risk pool, the more cost-efficiently the entities function.

Reinsurance companies purchase the risk from primary insurers. An insurance company may buy reinsurance on a proportional basis (sharing risk from the first dollar) or on an excess basis (over and above a certain limit). An excess basis is less expensive and more popular. Reinsurance companies allow purchasers to increase the amount of coverage they offer and spread their risk among a larger pool of applicants than they could otherwise afford. Reinsurers have grown in importance with the shift toward smaller, physician-owned insurance companies.

Joint underwriting associations and *patient compensation funds,* generally viewed as a last resort, are overseen or managed by states. In some instances, hospital systems also set up arrangements for their physicians who cannot obtain coverage elsewhere.

Some large practices and physician organizations have developed their own malpractice insurance captive company or have chosen to self-insure. Captives can be formed in 22 U.S. states and several other countries. All states have guaranteed funds in case their state-based insurance companies fail financially, but that is not true of foreign-based captives. Start-up capital needed to form a captive is estimated to be $1 million to $3 million. The risks of captive companies include: the risk that the company may become insolvent, the risk that hospitals could object to physicians forming their own insurance coverage, and the risk that the captive will have to purchase reinsurance.

Self-insurance plans generally demand less set-up time and up-front costs but may be managed by someone with less knowledge in the field. The difficulty is in determining how much to save in the plan because money set aside could be deemed an asset for the taking in a malpractice suit. They must also be structured to avoid connection with the physicians' assets, so the assets cannot be accessed during a suit.

There are various resources to help you evaluate existing companies, including company filings with state agencies and insurance rating companies such as A.M. Best Company (www.ambest.com).

Sources:

Matthew Vuletich, "Quick Tip: Captive Insurance Companies and Self-Insurance: Don't Expect the Benefits Without the Burdens," *MGMA e-Connexion*, Issue 96, March 2006.

Matthew Vuletich, "Quick Tip: OB/GYN Group Forms Captive Company to Stabilize Insurance Premiums," *MGMA e-Connexion*, April 2004, www.mgma.com/article.aspx?id=7442 (accessed August 9, 2006).

I want to take action against insurance carriers that do not honor their contract payment deadlines (typically 30 or 45 days) on clean claims or that delay reimbursement in other ways. What recourse do I have?

Your first step should be to review your state's prompt-payment law. When insurers' tactics for delaying reimbursement to physicians became an increasing burden on health care providers, most states passed regulations requiring prompt payment. You will need to understand the specifics of the applicable state regulation in terms of defining "clean claims," how the insurer can determine time for payment, the types of payers covered, and the applicability of the law based on the payer's location. The law may include requirements for paying interest or a fine per claim for any violations.

Before approaching the payer, you should review your claims and reimbursement time with the definitions in your state's statutes. Does the insurer calculate time to process your claim based on the date you submit the claim or the date they receive the claim? Are your claims clean according to the definition? Also, review your contract with the payer. Are there any hidden terms that may affect your challenge? Are you prepared to drop the contract with the payer, or does it represent a large percentage of your revenue?

You may want to contact your local MGMA chapter or your state medical society for assistance in locating and understanding the regulation and identifying other practices that are facing the same issue with the same payer. There may be options for approaching the payer as a group.

Next, contact the payer to begin negotiation. If the company representative has been unresponsive, contact the provider's relations department head or its compliance and legal departments. Negotiation is usually cheaper than legal recourse and can be as effective.

Other steps you can take to improve payer response include the following:

- ➤ Review your claims submission process to ensure the claims are accurate the majority of the time. Switch to an electronic claims submission process if you haven't already.

- ➤ Get organized. Document all the denials and delays, your responses, and the payers' replies. Keep track of every step in the process.

- ➤ Talk to other providers and encourage them to get involved. There is strength in numbers.

- ➤ Form an action group with other practice and health care administrators.

- ➤ Meet with employers in your area and explain your situation. Chances are that human resources directors have heard only the insurance industry's side of the story.

- Make sure that your state has the following regulations protecting providers' interests:

  - They require payers to fully disclose all contracted rates for any procedure;

  - They require payers to use nationally recognized coding terminology and procedures, including the use of modifiers and the Centers for Medicare & Medicaid Services Common Procedure Coding System; and

  - They require prompt payment, with enforceable penalties and fines for unethical stalling tactics.

- As a last resort, consider filing a lawsuit.

Provider lawsuits against payers have been successful. In 2005, three insurers – Health Net, Prudential, and WellPoint – agreed to settle allegations raised by a group of state and county medical societies of improper or illegal reimbursements. Among other terms, the insurers agreed to:

- Modify the definition of medical necessity;

- Cease using claims-processing software that modifies claims from their original service code designations;

- Pay electronic claims within 15 days of receipt and paper claims within 30 days; and

- Provide an electronic fee schedule.

Armed with the knowledge of state regulations, experiences of other providers with the payer, and knowledge of previous physician successes, you should be ready to challenge the payer.

Sources:

MGMA Government Affairs Department, "Washington Report: Additional Settlements Reached in Managed Care Litigation," *MGMA e-Connexion,* Issue 82, August 2005.

CHAPTER 8: Risk Management   **259**

Robert L. Roth and Margrit H Nahra, "Knowledge Is Payment: Understanding State Prompt-Payment Laws," *Healthcare Financial Management*, V. 55, No. 5, May 2001.

Joyce Vollmer, "Insights: Battling Whack-o-Nomics: Fighting for the Money You Have Earned," *MGMA Connexion*, V. 3, No. 7, August 2003, www3.mgma.com/articles/index.cfm?fuseaction=detail.main&articleID=12540 (accessed August 11, 2006).

My team is looking for ideas for making our practice more welcoming to our disabled patients. Do you have any ideas? What are other practices doing?

You are to be congratulated on recognizing the special needs of some of your patients. Your practice can take several steps to ensure it can accommodate and welcome these patients. The actual requirements from your practice will vary according to the needs of the individual patients:

➤ Identify patients with special medical needs. When they come for an appointment, prepare any additional requirements that may be needed to assist them during the appointment time (such as extra medical assistants, translators, or exam room preparation).

➤ Recognize that patients with special needs often have several medical issues and may require lengthier appointments.

➤ Allow families to be part of the medical process and decision making. They are usually heavily involved in the patient's care and know their health care issues intimately.

➤ All practices are required to comply with the Americans with Disabilities Act (ADA), but you can look into additional strategies to enhance your practice's facilities. Can your reception/waiting areas

FOR MORE INFORMATION...

Websites with additional information:
- ✔ Americans with Disabilities Act (ADA) home page, U.S. Department of Justice, www.usdoj.gov/crt/ada
- ✔ ADA & IT Technical Assistance Centers, www.adata.org
- ✔ Developmental Disabilities: Resources for Healthcare Providers, www.ddhealthinfo.org
- ✔ The Institute for Family-Centered Care, www.familycenteredcare.org
- ✔ Pediatric Alliance PC, www.pediatricalliance.com

---

and hallways easily accommodate a wheelchair? Is at least one exam table low enough for a wheelchair user? Are there enough electrical outlets in exam rooms so that patients using medical equipment can recharge their batteries during the visit? Do you include literature addressing special-needs patients in your reception area? Immuno-compromised patients should not be required to wait in the waiting area with a roomful of sick patients.

➤ Include all applicable diagnosis codes during each visit, regardless of the reason for the exam. This coding helps show the acuity of these patients and why they need more time.

➤ Keep handy the up-to-date emergency information form for each special-needs patient. You never know when you may need it. Provide copies to the hospital, the family, and the patient's school or job so that emergency medical personnel will understand the basics of their needs.

➤ Provide your staff with training on working with special-needs patients and ensure that they are committed to turning your practice into a welcoming medical home.

Source:

"Quick Tip: Fine-Tune Your Practice to Accommodate Special-Needs Patients," *MGMA e-Connexion*, Issue 25, February 2003.

QUESTION 98

One of my new physicians wants to know if she should become a Medicare participating provider. What are the advantages and disadvantages? Can she limit the number of Medicare or Medicaid patients or patient appointments on her schedule?

If your physician enrolls with Medicare, she agrees to become a participating provider and accept Medicare's reimbursement rates as payment in full. As an incentive for providers to participate in the program, Medicare reimburses her services at 100 percent of the approved rate for any given service, pays more rapidly than nonparticipating providers, and includes her in the directory of Medicare providers. Participating providers receive 80 percent of this payment from Medicare and 20 percent from the patient. Physicians are allowed to change their participation on an annual basis.

If your physician chooses to not participate (nonpar) in Medicare, she has the option to accept assignment. If the nonpar provider accepts assignment, Medicare pays claims at 95 percent of the participating amount, with 80 percent of that amount coming from the carrier and 20 percent from the patient. If the nonpar provider decides not to accept assignment, she must fill out a Medicare beneficiary's claim form and submit the claim directly to Medicare. Medicare then pays the patient directly, leaving the physician to bill the patient for services rendered. Physicians cannot charge Medicare patients for filing their claims, but by refusing assignment, nonpar physicians can balance-bill patients up to the limiting charge.

Federal law restricts Medicare nonparticipating providers from balance-billing more than 115 percent of the Medicare nonparticipating reimbursement rate. This is called the "limiting charge." Additionally, several states have enacted limiting charges. Effectively, the Medicare limiting charge translates into 109.25 percent of the participating amount, so a nonparticipating physician can, theoretically, realize higher income than a participating provider. This can only happen, however, if the majority of patients meet their financial obligations. In addition, the revenue stream will be slowed as practices wait for patients to reimburse them, and practices may incur expenses as a result of increased administrative work.

Physicians may also choose to stay out of the Medicare system entirely. You can then bill patients directly for their services at rates agreed to with the patient. To meet the legal requirements for the opt-out option, a physician must sign and file an affidavit agreeing not to bill or receive payment from the Medicare program for at least two years. This includes direct, indirect, or capitated payments. Indirect payments could come from an organization that receives direct or capitated payments from Medicare.

The physician must file this affidavit at least 30 days before the first day of the next calendar quarter and may rescind the affidavit within 90 days of the affidavit's effective date. The physician and Medicare patient must sign a written contract before rendering any service. The contract must clearly state that by signing the contract the beneficiary:

> ➤ Gives up all Medicare payments for services rendered by the contracting physician;

CHAPTER 8: Risk Management

➤ Is liable for all charges without Medicare balance billing limitations or assistance from Medigap or other supplemental insurance; and

➤ Acknowledges that the beneficiary has the right to receive services from medical providers eligible for Medicare coverage.

Regarding the question about limiting the number of appointments for Medicare enrollees, Robert Saner II, Esq., MGMA member and Washington counsel, Powers Pyles Sutter & Verville PC, Washington, D.C., provides the following advice:

> There is no generally applicable federal law or regulation that requires a physician or group to accept Medicare or Medicaid patients, or to take all Medicare patients if some are accepted. Similarly, state laws are generally silent with respect to the issue. Thus, in the absence of insurance contract provisions applicable in individual situations, many groups have historically used scheduling practices to limit the number of patients from one or more payor classes, which may include Medicare or Medicaid.
>
> There are, however, situations where restrictive scheduling policies can be problematic. For example, if a physician does treat Medicare or Medicaid patients, s/he can be sanctioned if that treatment does not meet "professionally recognized standards of health care." (Section 1128(b)(6)(B) of the Social Security Act.) Failure to promptly schedule diagnostic tests or procedures, or follow-up visits, for existing Medicare patients in a manner that effectively produces lower quality care than the practice provides to other payor classes could violate this provision.

Similarly, Medicare managed care plans generally have obligations to provide reasonable and necessary care to their enrollees, and these obligations are generally passed through to practices with which they contract directly or through PPOs and IPAs. If restrictive scheduling practices effectively restrict access, the practice may be in violation of contract provisions to which it has agreed.

Other examples include hospital systems that have certain charity care obligations by virtue of Hill-Burton funding, tax-exempt practices that have community benefit obligations, state university based academic practices that have "mission-based" restrictions on their ability to discriminate against Medicaid or other under-insured populations, ventures that seek compliance with kickback law "safe harbors," which sometimes impose nondiscrimination requirements, and organizations operating under corporate integrity agreements that include requirements that go beyond basic law and regulation.

Finally, payer-derived scheduling practices could in some circumstances look like race or age-based discrimination that runs afoul of state and federal civil rights laws to which some but not all practices are subject.

In short, this is a very complicated area of the law, and groups should proceed with caution when establishing restrictive scheduling practices.

Source:

Medical Group Management Association, Government Affairs Department, "Medicare Participation Decision FAQs," www.mgma.com/members/advocacy/medparticipationfaq.cfm (accessed August 11, 2006).

Robert Saner II, Esq., Powers Pyles Sutter & Verville PC, Washington, D.C., e-mail communication, November 8, 2006.

QUESTION 99

Are there any Stark, fraud and abuse, or antikickback issues regarding the rental or lease of office space from other doctors? We would like to rent some office space in another doctor's office, on a part-time basis.

There is concern about violating antikickback regulations if your practice and the office space owners refer patients to each other. The Office of Inspector General (OIG) of the U.S. Department of Health and Human Services issued a Special Fraud Alert on "Rental of Space in Physician Offices by Persons or Entities to Which Physicians Refer." The OIG acknowledged that there are rental arrangements that are appropriate for the parties involved and, therefore, are legal.

The Fraud Alert announced the following specifics that would be scrutinized:

> ➤ The rental agreements must be appropriate. If rent is suddenly being charged for space that had traditionally been offered for free or for a nominal fee, the rent would be considered suspect.

> ➤ Rental amounts must be at fair market value and not based on the volume of referrals between the two parties. Rent must not exceed that of the primary lease holders or be subject to adjustments more than once a year.

> ➤ The space that is being rented must not be in excess of the lessee's needs or for more time than it is needed. Excess rental payments may be considered as payments for referrals.

To ensure that your arrangement is within the guidelines of the "safe harbor" for rental agreements, follow these criteria from the Fraud Alert:

> ➤ The agreement is set out in writing and signed by the parties;

- ➤ The agreement covers all of the premises rented by the parties for the term of the agreement and specifies the premises covered by the agreement;

- ➤ If the agreement is intended to provide the lessee with access to the premises for periodic intervals rather than on a full-time basis, the rental agreement must state exactly the schedule of such intervals, their precise length, and the exact rent for such intervals;

- ➤ The term of the rental agreement is not less than one year;

- ➤ The aggregate rental charge is set in advance and is consistent with fair market value, and it is not determined in a manner that takes into account the volume or value of any referrals or business otherwise generated between the parties; and

- ➤ The total space rented does not exceed that which is reasonably necessary to accomplish the business purpose of the rental.

Sources:

Michael A. Dowell and Andrew G. Russell, "OIG Urges Review of Physician Office Space Rental Arrangements," *Group Practice Journal*, V. 49, No. 6, June 2000.

Kent J. Moore, "Is Your Space Rental Arrangement Fraudulent?" *Family Practice Management*, V. 7, No. 7, July/August 2000.

QUESTION 100

One of my physicians wants to start notifying patients of their test results using e-mail. What are the ethical and legal concerns with regard to the use of e-mail?

HIPAA regulations do not restrict communicating with patients using e-mail as long as steps are taken to ensure that patient protected health information (PHI) is not inappropriately disclosed. It is advisable to obtain a signed consent form and notify the patient that you may be communicating the test results via e-mail. E-mail should not be used to communicate abnormal or indeterminate test results. Use e-mail only for delivering good news.

The following steps should be taken to ensure that e-mail communication is done securely and appropriately:

- Require that patient communication messages are only sent through the practice's e-mail system.

- Work with your e-mail provider and Internet service provider (ISP) to understand the security options of your current system. Investigate encryption options to increase security.

- Include a statement regarding the group's e-mail communication policies in your Privacy Notice.

- Have patients sign a statement that they are interested in receiving practice communications via e-mail, and either copy or scan it into the patient's chart. The statement should outline appropriate use of e-mail by the patient and the practice.

- Protect PHI by double-checking e-mail addresses in patient files and before sending any e-mail message. Never forward a message with PHI unless consent has been received from the patient.

- Save all e-mail communications and file them with the patient's medical record.

- Develop an automatic reply to acknowledge receipt of the e-mail message, specifying within which time frame they will receive a reply. Provide a phone number for emergency contact or for when a reply is not received within the specified time frame.

- Include in each e-mail message a privacy and confidentiality statement.

You should develop a policy including these guidelines and require compliance from every employee and physician. The policy should also outline appropriate and inappropriate uses of e-mail for patient communication.

The MGMA *Operating Policies & Procedures Manual,* by Elizabeth W. Woodcock, MBA, FACMPE, CPC, includes a comprehensive example of an e-mail communication policy.

Sources:

"Establish Rules for Your E-mail Messages," *Private Practice Success,* January 2003.

Mark Meyer, "Physician Use of E-mail: The Telephone of the 21st Century," *Journal of Medical Practice Management,* V. 19, No. 5, March/April 2004.

Joseph E. Scherger, "Communicating With Your Patients Online," *Family Practice Management,* V. 11, No. 3, March 2004.

QUESTION 101

Where can we obtain a template for a business associate agreement and other forms for HIPAA compliance?

Several products are available that contain sample forms related to HIPAA compliance, along with information on their context. The following products are available from MGMA (www.mgma.com):

➤ *HIPAA Toolbox: Information Critical to Your Practice,* 2nd Edition, by Robert M. Tennant and Aaron N. Krupp, 2003 (with Standards for Electronic Security, 2004 supplement), Item #5913;

➤ *Organizing for HIPAA Compliance,* Three-part CD series, 2003, Item #5944; and

➤ *Operating Policies & Procedures Manual for Medical Practices,* by Elizabeth Woodcock and Bette Warn, 2006, Item #6495.

You can also conduct an Internet search to identify other products and online resources. The Website for the Office for Civil Rights of the U.S. Department of Health & Human Services, HIPAA, includes a business associate contract at www.hhs.gov/ocr/hipaa.

INDEX

A

Accounts payable, management guidelines for, 36–37
Accounts receivables
 bad debts and, 59–60
 buy-in structure and, 131
 financial assessment of practice based on, 54
 management of, 33–34
Advanced access system
 appointments management using, 21–22
 minimization of cancellations and no-shows and, 6
Advertising, budget development for, 192–194
Amatayakul, Margaret, 161–163
American College of Medical Practice Executives (ACMPE), 2
 board certification procedures, 213–214
 Body of Knowledge for Medical Practice Management, 222–224, 231–233
 Code of Medical Ethics, 228
American Health Information Management Association, 60–61
 medical records storage, 172–173
American Medical Association, Code of Medical Ethics, 228
Americans with Disabilities Act (ADA)
 disabled patient guidelines, 259–260
 translator/interpreter services regulations, 237–238
American Translators Association, 238
Ancillary services, revenue development with, 200–202

Antikickback regulations
 ancillary services and, 202
 office rental or lease, 264–266
Application service providers (ASPs), guidelines for using, 169–171
Appointment capacity, assessment of, 21–22
Appointment reminder techniques, 5–6
Appointment systems, advanced access techniques and, 21–22
Arbitration provisions, in employment agreements, 135
Assessment Manual, 8
Assessment procedures
 board of directors performance evaluation, 84–86
 practice operations, 7–9
Asset assessment, buy-in structure and, 131

B

Backlog of appointments, reduction of, 21–22
Bad debt management, guidelines for, 58–60
Behavioral management issues
 code of conduct development guidelines, 226–229
 physician behavior, 140–142
Billing services
 centralized *vs.* decentralized billing offices, 49–50
 for high-deductible plan patients, 66–67
 in house *vs.* outsourcing of, 38–39
 productivity assessment of, 51–52

Billing Service Selection Checklist, 39
Board certification procedures, 213–214
Boards of directors
  duties and responsibilities of, 76–79
  performance evaluation of, 83–86
Body of Knowledge for Medical Practice Management, domains of, 2
"Buddy system," for new physicians, 123–124
Budget development
  marketing and advertising needs, 192–194
  new physician recruitment and, 113–115
Business and clinical operations
  appointment systems, advanced access techniques, 21–22
  assessment areas in medical practice, 7–9
  facility expansion, lease *vs.* ownership of, 12–14
  facility space data and planning, 24–26
  financial performance studies, 16–18
  nonphysician hiring criteria, 10–11
  patient communication improvement, 22–24
  patient flow changes and improvements, 18–21
  patient no-shows and late cancellations, 5–7
  patient turnover and retention, 14–15
  patient waiting times and delays, 26–28
  physician hiring criteria, 10–11
  physician productivity and space efficiency, 29–30
Business associate agreements, resources for, 268

Business skills, practice administrators' knowledge of, 218–219
Buy-in structure, development of, 129–131
Bylaws, requirements for, 75–76

C

"Care teams," checkout process using, 20
Centers for Medicare & Medicaid Services, 172–173
Centralized billing offices, benefits and disadvantages of, 49–50
Certified Medical Practice Executive (CMPE), benefits of, 213–214
Changes in organization, preparation and implementation of, 92–95
Charge capture, for PDAs, 151–153
Charge tickets, patient flow improvement and management of, 19–20
Chart of Accounts for Health Care, financial assessment of practice based on, 58
Checking accounts, accounts payable management and review of, 37
Check-in process, minimization waiting times and appointment delays and, 27–28
Checkout process, patient flow improvement and, 18–20
Chief executive officer (CEO)
  incentive/bonus system for, 109–111
  leadership development and, 82
Citizenship principle, 229
Claims follow-up
  bad debts and, 59–60
  reimbursement delays and, 256–259
Claims rejections
  bad debt from, 58–60

management and reduction of, 62–63
Cleveland Clinic Foundation (CCF), 9
Code of conduct, development guidelines for, 226–229
Coding productivity
  Current Procedural Technology codes, 61
  improvement strategies for, 60–61
Collaborative relationships, evaluation of, 85
Collection agencies, contracts with, 39–40
Collection procedures, for high-deductible plan patients, 66–67
Collins, Hobart, 68
Commercial issues, board of directors' understanding of, 85–86
Commercial Law League of America, 40
Commercial payers, bad debt from, 58–60
Communications skills
  for practice administrators, 216–217
  public speaking and writing skills, 220–222
Compensation
  in buy-in structures, 130–131
  EHR technology and improvements in, 165
  for emergency room calls, 68–71
  employee courtesy discounts, guidelines for, 244–246
  employee salary data sources, 132
  in employment agreements, 132–136
  incentive/bonus systems, 108–111
  for managing partners, 91–92
  partner buyouts for retiring physicians, 99–101
  for part-time physicians, 128–129
  of physicians, model for, 136–140
  production-based *vs.* guaranteed salary structure, 111–112
  start-up costs of new practices and, 43
Competency-based reviews, employee performance evaluation using, 146
Computer-assisted real-time transcription (CART) services, 237–238
Computer systems
  IT policies for employee use of, 156–160
  RFP guidelines for purchase of, 153–155
Computer viruses, IT use policies and, 158
Conduct. *See* Behavioral management issues
Conflict resolution, physician behavior issues and, 141–142
Contractual write-offs, bad debt from, 58–60
Copyright protection, IT use policies and, 158
Cost Survey Report
  accounts receivables guidelines, 33
  billing service costs, 39
  facility space data and planning, 24–25
  financial performance evaluations, 16
  multispecialty practices and, 205–207
  number of FTE staff per physician data, 124–127
  physician hiring criteria and, 10–11
  practice financial performance data in, 57–58
  staffing ratios in, 126–127

Courtesy discounts for employees, guidelines for, 244–246
Current Procedural Terminology (CPT) codes
  fee schedule development and, 53–54
  responsibilities for, 61

D

Data backup procedures, off-site storage systems, 167–168
Data confidentiality, IT use policies and, 158
Data gathering guidelines, physician behavior issues, 142
Date of service cycle times, financial assessment of practice based on, 54–55
Decentralized billing offices, benefits and disadvantages of, 49–50
Deferred compensation, in partner buyouts, 99
Delayed appointments, strategies for avoiding, 26–28
Delinquent accounts, collection agencies and, 40
Denied claims. *See* Claims rejections
Department of Health and Human Services (DHSS), 238
Developmental Disabilities: Resources for Healthcare Providers (Website), 260
Dignity principle, 228–229
Disabled patients, practice management guidelines for, 259–260
Disaster and recovery plans, resources for development of, 246–250
Discount policies, practice management strategies concerning, 63–65
Diversification of services, revenue development with, 200–202
Due diligence principle, merger planning and, 185

E

Economies of scale, mergers and, 184–186
Educational materials
  patient flow improvement and distribution of, 20
  for physician leaders, 82
Electronic Health Records: Transforming Your Medical Practice, 161–163
Electronic health records (EHR) system
  implementation strategies for, 92–95
  integration with EMR system, 150–151
  outsourcing of, 170–171
  ownership policies concerning, 171–172
  patient access guidelines, 176–177
  return-on-investment (ROI) analysis of, 160–165
  storage guidelines for, 172–173
  transcription system compatibility, 175–176
Electronic medical records (EMR) systems
  ownership policies concerning, 171–172
  patient access guidelines, 176–177
  return-on-investment analysis for purchase of, 164–165
  selection criteria for, 149–151
  storage guidelines for, 172–173
E-mail
  IT use policies concerning, 159
  test results notification using, 266–268
Emergency room calls, physician compensation for, 68–71
Employee performance reviews, development of, 143–146

Employee security, disaster plan development and issues of, 247
Employee turnover
    cost calculations and ratios for, 105–108
    medical records ownership policy and, 171–172
    physician retention strategies, 116–124
    rates for doctors, 123
Employment agreements
    courtesy discounts in, 244–246
    guidelines for, 132–136
    IT computer use policies and, 156–160
    medical records ownership, 171–172
Encounter forms, patient flow improvement and use of, 20
Ethics
    codes of, development guidelines, 226–229
    dismissal of noncompliant patients, 239–241
    for practice administrators, 231–233
Exit interviews, employee turnover data and, 106–108
Expenses, guidelines for calculating, 35–36
External research, vs. internal research, 183

F

Fabrizio, Nick, 79, 94, 113, 123
Facility design and expansion
    assessment resources for, 24–26
    lease vs. ownership issues, 12–14
    medical records storage issues, 172–173
    physician productivity maximization and, 29–30
    urgent care centers, 194–197
Fair-market value
    of medical practices, 41–42
    physician compensation for emergency room calls and, 68–71
Fairness principle, 229
Fee schedules
    information sources for, 53
    for new practices, 52–54
Fiduciary Principle, 227
Financial management
    accounts payable issues, 36–37
    accounts receivables and, 33–34
    bad debt management, 58–60
    billing service productivity, 51–52
    billing services, centralized vs. decentralized offices, 49–50
    billing services, in house vs. outsourcing, 38–39
    claims rejections, reduction and management of, 62–63
    code setting decisions, 61
    coding productivity, 60–61
    collection agencies, 39–40
    collections from high-deductibles patients, 65–67
    comparisons of operating costs/overhead, 57–58
    disaster plan development and security issues, 247–248
    emergency room call compensation, 68–71
    fair-market value determinations, 41–42
    fee schedule development, 52–54
    financial health assessment tools, 54–56
    physician hiring costs, 35–36
    start-up costs, 42–48
    uninsured patients, 63–65
Financial Management for Medical Groups: A Resource for New and Experience Managers, 34
Financial performance
    comparisons of practices and, 57–58

financial ratios and reports for assessment of, 54–56
practices for improvement in, 16–18
Financial ratios and reports, practice financial performance assessment and, 54–56
Financial reports, financial assessment of practice and, 55
Focus groups, market research using, 183
Fraud detection and management
space rental guidelines, 264–266
uninsured patients, 63–65
Full-time-equivalent (FTE) physicians
bad debts from FFS activities per, 59
median number of patients per, 10–11
performance indicators for, 17–18
practice size and hiring of, 205–207

G

Gans, David N., 125, 127
Geisinger Health System leadership case study, 82
Glass, Kathryn, 54
Goal-setting appraisals, employee performance evaluation using, 146
Governance and organizational dynamics
administrator-physician relationships, 88–91
board of directors performance evaluation, 83–86
board of directors responsibilities and duties, 76–79
bylaws development, 75–76
EHR implementation, 92–95
leadership development strategies, 80–83
managing partner compensation issues, 91–92

mission statement development, 86–88
Governing Policies Manual for Medical Practices, 78
codes of ethics and, 228
Graduate Medical Education National Advisory Committee (GMENAC), 187–188
Gross charges, trends in, 54
Guaranteed salary plans, for new physicians, 111–112

H

Handheld computers, implementation strategies for, 151–153
Hansen, Richard D., 80–81
Health care environment, practice administrators' knowledge of, 218
Healthcare Information and Management Systems Society, information technology resources, 166
Healthcare Leadership Alliance, 219
Health Insurance Portability and Accountability Act (HIPAA)
employee training in provisions of, 242–244
forms from, 268
PDA regulations, 153
Privacy Rule, 176–177
Standards for Electronic Security, 168
Health savings accounts (HSAs), collections strategies for patients with, 65–67
Hicks-Glenn study, 187–188
High-deductible plans, collections strategies for, 65–67
Hill-Burton hospital funding, 264
HIPAA Toolbox: Information Critical to Your Practice, 268
Hiring decisions
cost calculations for, 35–36

expansion criteria as basis for, 10–11
Honesty/truth principle, 228
Hospitals, physician compensation for emergency room calls at, 68–71
HR Policies & Procedures Manual for Medical Practices, 102
   IT policies in, 160
Human resources management
   buy-in structure for new physicians, 129–131
   employee performance evaluation, 143–146
   employee salary data sources, 132
   employee turnover costs and rates, 105–108, 116–118
   incentive/bonus system development, 108–111
   locum tenens physician hiring, 115–116
   new physician orientation checklist, 119–124
   part-time scheduling, 127–129
   physician behavior issues, 140–142
   physician compensation model, 136–140
   physician employment agreement guidelines, 132–136
   physician recruitment and compensation, 111–115
   physician retention strategies, 116–124
   practice administrator performance and incentives, 108–111
   retirement guidelines, 99–101
   rightsizing system for staffing of practices, 124–127
   sexual harassment policies, 102–105

I

Incentive/bonus system
   physician compensation plans, 137–140
   for practice administrators, 108–111
Incorporated practices, bylaws requirements, 76–77
Information Exchange
   #3410, 24
   #4237, 145
   #4294, 139
   #4742, 91–92
   #4879, 154–155
   #4880, 145
   #5986, 139
   #6673, 228
   administrator incentive plans, 108–111
   billing service practices, 38–39
   on collection agencies, 39–40
   for high-deductible plans, 66–67
   managing partner compensation, 91–92
Information management
   handheld computers and personal digital assistants, implementation, 151–153
   in-house *vs.* outsourced staffing for, 169–171
   IT policy development, 156–160
   IT system upgrades, 164–165
   management technology resources, 166–167
   medical records copying policies, 176–178
   medical records ownership issues, 171–172
   medical records storage management, 172–173
   off-site data storage, 167–168
   practice management system selection, 149–151

practice valuation with medical records, 178
request for proposal development, 153–155
return-on-investment analysis, 160–163
transcription services costs, 173–176
Institute for Family-Centered Care, 260
Insurance captives, malpractice coverage through, 254–255
Internal research, *vs.* external research, 183
Internet
  employee computer use policy for, 157–160
  information technology resources on, 167
Interviews, market research using, 183
IT Return on Investment Calculator, 163

J

Johnson, Bruce A., 99
Joint underwriting associations, malpractice coverage through, 255
Joint ventures, Stark regulations concerning, 241–242

K

Kaplan, Gary, 90–91
Keegan, Deborah Walker, 51, 125–126
Krupp, Aaron N., 268

L

Late cancellations, reduction strategies for, 5–7
Leadership development
  medical practice management, 215–219
  for physician leaders, 80–83

Leased facilities, benefits and drawbacks of, 12–14
Legal and ethical issues, organizational understanding of, 85
Legislative issues, in medical practice, 230–231
Limited English proficiency (LEP) regulations, 238
Locum tenens physicians, hiring and billing practices using, 115–116

M

Mail surveys
  market research using, 183
  patient loyalty assessment using, 191–192
Malkin, Jain, 25
Malpractice coverage
  cost reduction strategies for, 253–256
  in employment agreements, 132–136
Management Compensation Survey 2005 Report, 92
Management services organizations (MSOs), advantages and disadvantages of, 208–210
Managing partners, compensation for, 91–92
Market-based compensation, for emergency room calls by specialists, 68–71
Marketing
  budget for, 192–194
  management services organization contracts, 208–210
  market research guidelines, 181–184
  mergers of medical groups, 184–186
  patient loyalty surveys, 189–192
  physician hiring increases, 205–207

physician needs assessment, data sources for, 186–189

referral increases, strategies for, 203–204

revenue opportunities development, 200–202

strategic planning guidelines, 197–200

urgent care facilities development, 194–197

Market research, goals and guidelines for, 181–184

Market share, analysis of, 181–184

Masiello, John J., 162

Mastering Patient Flow, patient no-shows in, 5–6

Mastering Patient Flow: More Ideas to Increase Efficiency and Earnings, 18–19

Median number of patients, per FTE physicians, 11

Medical and Dental Space Planning: A Comprehensive Guide to Design, Equipment, and Clinical Procedures, 25

Medical Group Management Association (MGMA)

Code of Medical Ethics, 228

Government Affairs Department, 230–231

Information Center activities at, 1–2, v–vi

information technology resources, 166

strategic planning tools of, 198–199

Medical Performance Management Manual: How to Evaluate Employees, 145

Medical practices

fair-market value of, 41–42

start-up costs for, 42–48

Medical records. *See* Electronic health records (EHR) system; Electronic medical records system

Medicare Carrier Manual, 115–116

Medicare/Medicaid

locum tenens physician claims and, 115–116

medical records retention requirements, 172–173

pay-for-performance program of, 138

physician participation in, 261–264

Mergers, advantages and disadvantages of, 184–186

MGMA Connexion, 56

MGMA *Information Exchange,* patient no-shows and late cancellation data in, 5

Minute clinics. *See* Urgent care centers

Missed appointments, charges for, 5–6

Mission statement, development of, 86–88

Monitoring techniques, for no-shows, 6

Multispecialty practices

guidelines for developing, 205–207

performance indicators for, 17–18

N

National Association for Ambulatory Urgent Care (NAFAC), 196

National Center for Healthcare Statistics, 182

Needs assessment

financial assessment of practice and, 55–56

number of physicians, determination of, 186–189

practice management system selection, 149–151

Nelson, Rosemarie, 54

Network security, IT use policies and, 158–159

New physicians
  buy-in structure for, 129–131
  cost calculations for hiring of, 35–36
  criteria for hiring, 10–11
  employment agreement for, 132–136
  growth of collections data for, 43
  orientation checklist for, 119–124
  recruitment strategies for, 111–115
New practices
  checklist for start-up of, 44–48
  fee schedule for, 52–54
  start-up costs for, 42–43
Nguyen, Loc, 49–50
Noncompete covenants, in employment agreements, 135
Noncompliant patients, dismissal of, 239–241
Novak, Alys, 78, 145, 160

O

Office hours, waiting times and appointment delays and extension of, 27–28
Office of Inspector General (OIG)
  employee courtesy discount guidelines, 244–246
  joint venture regulations, 241–242
  locum tenens physicians hiring and, 116
  space rental guidelines, 264–266
Off-site data storage, guidelines for, 167–168
On-call specialists, stipend data for, 69–71
Operating costs/overhead
  financial assessment of practice based on, 55
  in multispecialty practices, 205–207
  practice financial performance evaluation and, 57–58
Operating policies and procedures, documentation requirements for, 18–20
Operating Policies & Procedures Manual for Medical Practices
  e-mail notification of test results, 267–268
  employee computer use guidelines, 156–160
  HIPAA compliance forms, 268
  HIPAA training guidelines, 244
Organizational culture
  board of directors' knowledge of, 85
  employee retention and, 107–108
Organizing for HIPAA Compliance, 268
Orientation program, as physician retention tool, 118–124
Ortiz, Cesar, 56
Outsourcing
  of billing services, 38–39
  of information technology functions, 169–171
  of transcription services, 173–176
Ownership of facilities, benefits and drawbacks of, 12–14

P

Partner buyout, guidelines for, 99–101
Part-time scheduling, for physicians, 127–129
Patient access
  assessment of, 8
  disabled patient guidelines, 259–260
  to medical records, 176–177
Patient care programs, PDA technology and, 152
Patient communication
  e-mail notification of test results, 266–268

improvement strategies for, 22–24
mitigation of waiting times and appointment delays and, 28
Patient compensation funds, malpractice coverage through, 255
Patient dismissals, noncompliant patients, 239–241
Patient education, for high-deductible plans, 65–67
Patient flow, improvement strategies for, 18–20
Patient loyalty
strategies for building, 6
surveys for assessment of, 189–192
Patient no-shows, reduction strategies for, 5–7
Patient per hour (PPH) rates, physician productivity maximization and, 29–30
Patient retention and turnover
data on, 14–15
strategies for managing, 15
Patient safety, disaster plan development and issues of, 246–247
Patient satisfaction surveys
case study using, 192
communication issues and, 22–24
loyalty assessment using, 189–192
waiting times and appointment delays and, 27–28
Patient visits
alternatives to, 22
start-up costs and growth and number data on, 43
Patterson, Sarah, 90–91
Pay-for-performance programs, in physician compensation plans, 138–140

Payment process, patient flow improvement and guidelines for, 19–20
Pediatric Alliance, 260
Peer review, employee performance evaluation using, 144
Peer review process, development guidelines for, 250–253
Performance and Practices of Successful Medical Groups
accounts receivables guidelines, 33
claims rejection management and reduction, 62–63
employee turnover rates and, 105–108
financial performance evaluation guidelines, 16–17, 54
number of FTE staff per physician data, 124–127
Performance evaluation
accounts receivables as basis for, 34
for boards of directors, 83–86
buy-in structure as tool for, 129–131
employee performance reviews, 143–146
financial performance of practice, 16, 57–57
incentive/bonus system measures and, 110
in physician compensation plans, 137–140
of practice operations, 8–9
Performance wheel, practice operations assessment with, 8–9
Personal digital assistants (PDAs), implementation strategies for, 151–153
Peterson, Thomas P., 246–250
Physician Compensation: Models for Aligning Financial Goals and Incentives, 139

Physician Compensation and Production Survey, 10–11
Physician Compensation Plans: State-of-the-Art Strategies, 139
Physician employment agreements, retirement provisions in, 101
Physician mutual companies, malpractice coverage through, 253–254
"Physician Recruitment Update" (video), 117
Physicians. *See also* Full-time-equivalent (FTE) physicians; New physicians
  behavioral management issues involving, 140–142, 226–228
  buy-in structures for, 129–131
  compensation model for, 136–140
  Current Procedural Terminology (CPT) code responsibilities, 61
  group size and number of, 205–207
  hiring, expansion criteria for, 10–11
  hiring, waiting times and appointment delays as criteria for, 27–28
  leadership development programs for, 80–83
  locum tenens physicians, 115–116
  as managing partners, 91–92
  medical records ownership issues for, 171–172
  Medicare/Medicaid participation guidelines, 261–264
  need for, techniques for determining, 186–189
  number of FTE staff per, 124–127
  part-time scheduling for, 127–129
  practice administrators' relations with, 88–91
  productivity maximization of, 29–30
  referrals from, 203–204
  retention plan for keeping, 116–124
  retirement guidelines for, 99–101
Physician satisfaction survey, as retention tool, 123–124
Physician stock companies, malpractice coverage through, 253
Physician-to-population rations, physician needs assessment using, 187–189
Physician trusts, malpractice coverage through, 254
Planning procedures
  budget for, 192–194
  management services organization contracts, 208–210
  market research guidelines, 181–184
  mergers of medical groups, 184–186
  patient loyalty surveys, 189–192
  physician hiring increases, 205–207
  physician needs assessment, data sources for, 186–189
  referral increases, strategies for, 203–204
  revenue opportunities development, 200–202
  strategic planning guidelines, 197–200
  urgent care facilities development, 194–197
Positioning research, 183
Practice administrators
  board certification for, 213–214
  education resources on information technology for, 166–167
  ethical issues for, 231–233

incentive/bonus system for, 108–111
leadership development for, 215–219
physician leaders relations with, 88–91
professional growth strategies for, 222–224
stress management for, 224–226
uninsured patients guidelines, 63–64
Practice management reports, financial assessment of practice and, 55–56
Practice management systems, selection criteria for, 149–151
Practice operations
assessment of, 7–9
disaster plan development and capability assessment of, 248–249
rightsizing strategies for, 124–127
Practice size, mergers and issues of, 184–186
Practice Transition Self-Assessment Tool, 101
Practice valuations, medical records included in, 178
Prescription management programs, PDA technology and, 152
Price, Courtney, 145, 160
Primary care physicians, referrals from, 203–204
Privacy issues
e-mail notification of test results, 266–268
IT use policies and limitations on, 159
medical records copying policies, 176–177
Production-based compensation plans, for new physicians, 111–112
Productivity assessments

billing services, 51–52
coding productivity, 60–61
of new physicians, 35–36
physician productivity, 29–30
Professional associations, on information technology, 166–167
Professional growth, strategies for, 222–224
Professionalism, in practice administrators, guidelines for, 217–218
Professional responsibility
board certification process, 213–214
code ethics development guidelines, 226–229
ethical issues, 231–233
legislative and regulatory issues, 230–231
practice administrator stress management, 224–226
practice management leadership development, 215–219
professional growth strategies, 222–224
public speaking and writing skills development, 220–222
Property principle, 228
Protected health information (PHI), off-site data storage and, 168
Publications, information technology resources on, 167
Public speaking, skills development guidelines for, 220–222

Q

Quantitative *vs.* qualitative market research, 183–184
Quintana, Olga, 56

R

Reasonableness standard, physician compensation for emergency room calls and, 68–71

Reception area, mitigation of waiting times and appointment delays and, 28
Reciprocal insurers, malpractice coverage through, 254
Recruitment strategies
    employee retention and, 107–108
    for new physicians, 111–115
Referrals, patient flow improvement and paperwork for, 20
Regulatory issues
    in medical practice, 230–231
    Medicare/Medicaid participation, 262–264
    for peer review, 251–253
Reimbursement of claims, delays in, 256–259
Reinsurance companies, malpractice coverage through, 255
Relationship management skills, for practice administrators, 216–217
Relative value unit (RVU)
    fee schedule development and, 53–54
    physician compensation models, 139
Reliability principle, 228
Request for proposal (RFP)
    for computer systems, 153–155
    practice management system selection process, 150–151
    transcription systems, 175–176
Resource-based relative value scale (RBRVS), fee schedule development and, 52–54
Results assessment, patient loyalty surveys, 191–192
Retention of employees
    cost calculations and ratios for, 105–108
    physician retention strategies, 116–124
Retirement issues, guidelines for, 99–101

Return-on-investment (ROI) analysis
    electronic health records systems, 160–163
    IT system purchases, 164–165
    market share research and, 181–184
Revenue estimations, for new physicians, 35–36
Revenue opportunities, diversification of services and, 200–202
Rightsizing, strategies for, 124–127
Rightsizing: Appropriate Staffing for Your Medical Practice, 125
Risk management
    business associate agreements, 268
    disabled patient care, 259–261
    disaster and recovery plan development, 246–250
    e-mailing of test results, 266–268
    employee courtesy discounts, 244–246
    HIPAA requirements compliance, 242–244
    insurance reimbursement delays, 256–259
    in joint ventures, 241–242
    malpractice insurance costs, 253–256
    Medicare/Medicaid participation, 261–264
    noncompliant patients, 239–241
    office space rental or lease, 264–266
    peer review process, resources for, 250–253
    translator/interpreter services, 237–239
Risk retention groups (RRGs), malpractice coverage through, 254
RVUs: Applications for Medical Practice Success, 54

S

Safe harbor provisions
  joint ventures and, 241–242
  Medicare/Medicaid participation, 263–264
  space rental guidelines, 264–266
Salaries. *See* Compensation
Savings accounts, accounts payable management and review of, 37
Schaffer, Michael, 60
Scheduling strategies
  minimization of cancellations and no-shows and, 6
  waiting times and appointment delays, 26–28
Secret shoppers, market research using, 184
Segment-based market research, 183
Self-insurance plans, malpractice coverage through, 255–256
Self-paying patients
  bad debt from, 58–60
  practice management strategies for, 63–65
Sexual harassment policies, development guidelines for, 102–105
Single-specialty groups, number of FTE physicians in, 206–207
Sliding-scale fee programs, for uninsured patients, 65
Social Security Act, Medicare/Medicaid participation guidelines, 263–264
Space allocation and capacity. *See also* Facility design and expansion
  antikickback regulations concerning, 264–266
  new physician hiring and assessment of, 11
Specialist remuneration, compensation for emergency room calls and, 68–71
Speech/voice recognition systems, transcription using, 175–176
Staffing ratios, rightsizing strategies and, 124–127
Staff salary expenses, billing service costs, 39
Staff training programs, in Health Insurance Portability and Accountability Act provisions, 242–244
Staff workload assessments
  billing office productivity and, 51–52
  information technology staff, 169–171
  rightsizing strategies and, 124–127
Stark law, 202
  joint ventures and, 241–242
Start-up costs for practices, calculation of, 42–48
Strategic planning
  guidelines for developing, 197–199
  for mergers, 185
Strengths, weaknesses, opportunities, and threats (SWOT) analysis
  diversification of services based on, 202
  strategic planning using, 197–199
Stress management, for practice administrators, 224–226
Substance abuse, by physicians, 141–142
Successful Groups Cost Survey Supplement, 165
Supervisors duties, workplace harassment and, 103–105
Support staff
  hiring of, to minimize waiting times and appointment delays, 27–28
  number of FTE staff per physician, 124–127

T

Tablet-based charge capture system, 152–153

Telephone service, patient communication issues and, 23–24

Telephone surveys, market research using, 183

Tennant, Robert M., 268

Test results, e-mail notification of, 266–268

360-degree feedback technique, employee performance evaluation using, 146

Tilden, Nelson, 117

Time management tools, PDA technology and, 152

Time-of-service collection, for high-deductible plan patients, 66–67

Toastmasters International, 222

Transcription services
  computer-assisted real-time transcription (CART) services, 237–238
  in-house *vs.* outsourced cost comparisons, 173–176

Translator/interpreter services, regulations concerning, 237–238

U

Uninsured patients, practice management strategies concerning, 63–65

Urgent care centers, development guidelines for, 194–197

V

Value analysis research, 183

W

Waiting times, improvement strategies for, 26–28

Waiver policies, uninsured patients, 63–65

Walker, Deborah L., 139

Warn, Bette, 160, 268

Web-based market surveys, 183

Weiner study, 188–189

Woodcock, Elizabeth
  billing office productivity assessment by, 51–52
  on centralized *vs.* decentralized billing offices, 49–50
  e-mail communication policies, 267–268
  HIPAA compliance guidelines, 268
  on information technology, 160
  on patient no-shows and late cancellations, 5–6
  practice operations assessment tips, 7–9

Write-offs, uninsured patients, 64–65

Writing skills, development of, 220–222